D1349733

The Best of
BAKING

The Best of
BAKING

Annette Wolter and Christian Teubner

Photography by Christian Teubner

PEERAGE BOOKS

This edition published in 1991 by
Peerage Books
Michelin House
81 Fulham Road
London SW3 6RB

English edition first published by
The Hamlyn Publishing Group Limited
part of Reed International Books
© Copyright Reed International Books 1979

First published under the title
Back vergnügen wie noch nie
© Copyright by Gräfe und Unzer GmbH, München, 1978

All rights reserved. No part of this publication may be reproduced,
stored in a retrieval system, or transmitted, in any form or by any
means, electronic, mechanical, photocopying, recording or otherwise,
without the prior permission of the publishers and the copyrightholders.

ISBN 1 85052 207 3

The Publishers would like to thank Greens of Brighton for their
help and advice on the use of packet mixes in some of the recipes.

Phototypeset by Tradespools Ltd, Frome, Somerset

Produced by Mandarin Offset
Printed in Hong Kong

A catalogue record for this book is available from the British Library

Useful Facts and Figures

Notes on metrication

In this book quantities are given in metric and Imperial measures.
Because of the necessity for exact proportions in baking recipes, we
have not followed a standard conversion throughout but have carefully worked out and tested each recipe to the correct proportions
for that recipe. It is therefore especially important to follow *either*
the metric measures *or* the Imperial measures, never both.

Spoon measures All spoon measures given in this book, are level
unless otherwise stated.

Can sizes At present, cans are marked with the exact (usually to the
nearest whole number) metric equivalent of the Imperial weight of
the contents, so we have followed this practice when giving can sizes.

Flours Unless specified otherwise, plain flour has been used for all
the recipes in this book. Some of the more unusual flours e.g. maize
or rye flour, can be bought at health food or specialist food shops.

Vanilla sugar This is easily made (see page 234) or can be bought in
sachets.

Eggs Unless specified otherwise, the recipes in this book have been
tested using a size 3 egg; if you use smaller or larger eggs you may
need to adjust the recipe accordingly.

Yeast Fresh yeast has been used in almost all the recipes. If substi-
tuting dried yeast, use only half the specified amount and follow the
directions given on the package.

Quantities Many of the recipes in this book make very generous
quantities, as most cooks find it invaluable to make a large amount
and then freeze at least part of it.

Oven temperatures

The table below gives recommended equivalents.

	°C	°F	Gas Mark
Very cool	110	225	$\frac{1}{4}$
	120	250	$\frac{1}{2}$
Cool	140	275	1
	150	300	2
Moderate	160	325	3
	180	350	4
Moderately hot	190	375	5
	200	400	6
Hot	220	425	7
	230	450	8
Very hot	240	475	9

An Imperial / American guide to solid and liquid measures

Solid measures

IMPERIAL / *AMERICAN*
1 lb butter or margarine / *2 cups*
1 lb flour / *4 cups*
1 lb granulated or
  castor sugar / *2 cups*
1 lb icing sugar / *3 cups*

Liquid measures

IMPERIAL / *AMERICAN*
¼ pint liquid / *⅔ cup liquid*
½ pint / *1¼ cups*
¾ pint / *2 cups*
1 pint / *2½ cups*
1½ pints / *3¾ cups*
2 pints / *5 cups (2½ pints)*

NOTE: WHEN MAKING ANY OF THE RECIPES IN THIS BOOK, ONLY FOLLOW ONE SET OF MEASURES AS THEY ARE NOT INTERCHANGEABLE.

American terms

The list below gives some American equivalents or substitutes for terms and ingredients used in this book

Ingredients

BRITISH / *AMERICAN*
apple, cooking / *apple, baking*
apple purée / *applesauce*
bicarbonate of soda / *baking soda*
biscuits / *crackers or cookies*
biscuit mixture / *cookie dough*
black cherries / *bing cherries*
black treacle / *molasses*
cake mixture / *cake batter*
chocolate caraque / *chocolate
  curls*
chocolate, plain / *chocolate,
  semi-sweet*
chocolate vermicelli / *chocolate
  sprinkles*
cocoa powder / *unsweetened
  cocoa*
coconut, desiccated / *coconut,
  shredded*
cornflour / *cornstarch*
cream, single / *cream, light*
cream, double / *cream, heavy*
digestive biscuits / *Graham
  crackers*
essence / *extract*
flour, plain / *flour, all-purpose*
flour, self-raising / *flour, all-
  purpose sifted with baking
  powder*
gelatine / *gelatin*
glacé cherries / *candied cherries*
grapes, black / *grapes, purple*
grapes, green / *grapes, white*
icing / *frosting*
raisins, seedless / *raisins, seeded*
scones / *biscuits*
semolina / *semolina flour*
shortcrust pastry / *basic pie
  dough*
soured cream / *sour cream*
sponge finger biscuits / *lady-
  fingers*
sugar, icing / *sugar, confectioners'*
sultanas / *seedless white raisins*
vanilla pod / *vanilla bean*
yeast, fresh (25 g/1 oz) / *yeast,
  compressed (1 cake)*

Equipment and terms

BRITISH / *AMERICAN*
baking tray / *baking sheet*
base / *bottom*
cake board / *cake plate*
cling film / *saran wrap*
cocktail stick / *toothpick*
deep cake tin / *spring form pan*
double saucepan / *double boiler*
dough or mixture / *batter*
flan tin / *pie pan*
greaseproof paper / *wax paper*
knock back dough / *punch down
  dough*
liquidiser / *blender*
loaf tin / *loaf pan*
muslin / *cheesecloth*
palette knife / *spatula*
pastry or biscuit cutter / *cookie
  cutter*
pastry case / *pie shell*
patty or bun tins / *muffin pans
  or cups*
piping bag / *pastry bag*
polythene / *plastic*
prove dough / *rise dough*
pudding basin / *ovenproof bowl
  or pudding mold*
roasting tin / *roasting pan*
sandwich tin / *layer cake pan*
stoned / *pitted*
sugar thermometer / *candy
  thermometer*
Swiss roll tin / *jelly roll pan*
top and tail fruit / *stem fruit*
whisk eggs / *beat eggs*

Notes for American and Australian users

In America the 8-oz measuring cup is used. In Australia metric measures are now used in conjunction with the standard 250-ml measuring cup. The Imperial pint, used in Britain and Australia, is 20 fl oz, while the American pint is 16 fl oz. It is important to remember that the Australian tablespoon differs from both the British and American tablespoons; the table below gives a comparison. The British standard tablespoon, which has been used throughout this book, holds 17.7 ml, the American 14.2 ml, and the Australian 20 ml. A teaspoon holds approximately 5 ml in all three countries.

British	American	Australian
1 teaspoon	1 teaspoon	1 teaspoon
1 tablespoon	1 tablespoon	1 tablespoon
2 tablespoons	3 tablespoons	2 tablespoons
3½ tablespoons	4 tablespoons	3 tablespoons
4 tablespoons	5 tablespoons	3½ tablespoons

Contents

Introduction

The Best of Baking introduces you to over 350 of the best ever baking recipes. Each recipe has been fully tested and is illustrated with a beautiful colour photograph, enabling you to see how the finished cake, pastry or biscuit will look. This in itself is an encouragement as well as a tremendous time-saver, as you can appreciate at a glance all the finer details of decoration and garnish.

While choosing the recipes for this book, the following question came up: when do people bake and which recipes do they enjoy making most? The best known recipes have therefore been selected from the widest range available: old-time favourites, speciality recipes, as well as both traditional and modern ones, some for everyday and some for more special times. Such occasions as Christmas, New Year, Easter, family celebrations, parties and entertaining have been covered, giving you many new and unusual ideas. There is a section on cakes and gâteaux made with fruit, and for the health-conscious the chapter on wholemeal baking will prove more than satisfying. If you think a cake or gâteau looks too complicated, do not lose heart; start with the simpler recipes, progressing until you have successfully made even the most elaborate ones – do not set an upper limit for yourself. Practice will make you experienced and more confident, and help you to develop

different ideas. For years to come you will be baking all sorts of delights for friends and family – cakes, gâteaux, tartlets, pastries, biscuits and flans – and you will be surprised how quickly you develop your own ideas and slight variations that can make all the difference.

The section at the end of the book on the Art of Baking gives you much invaluable information on baking techniques and methods. It takes you through the basic recipes in clear and simple stages, so you can master these with confidence before moving on to the more elaborate cakes and gâteaux. Details of icing and decorating techniques are fully explained, so your finished cake will look every bit as professional as the illustration, and often with very little effort. There follows a glossary of baking ingredients, including several more unusual ingredients as well as everything needed to stock a basic store cupboard. Finally comes a section on baking for the freezer and a comprehensive freezing chart. This will prove invaluable to those of you who like to bake extra quantities and freeze the surplus.

So may we wish you much success in baking, pleasure in discovering your own favourite recipes and hope that you will enjoy baking, as well as the fruits of your labour, as never before.

Annette Wolter and Christian Teubner

Favourites Baked with Fruit

Blackberry Meringue Pie

PASTRY
200 g/7 oz plain flour
pinch of salt
100 g/3½ oz butter, cut into
  flakes
1 egg
2 tablespoons water
25 g/1 oz castor sugar
FILLING
350 g/12 oz blackberries
75 g/3 oz castor sugar
2 teaspoons cornflour
3 tablespoons gooseberry jam
MERINGUE
3 egg whites
175 g/6 oz castor sugar

Sift the flour and salt into a
bowl. Rub in the butter then
stir in the egg, water and sugar.
Form into a pastry dough,
wrap in foil or cling film and
leave for 2 hours in the
refrigerator.

Sprinkle the blackberries
with the sugar and leave to
drain in a sieve over a saucepan. Warm the berry juice.
Blend the cornflour with 1
tablespoon water, stir into the
berry juice, bring to the boil,
stirring, and simmer until
thickened. Add the blackberries
and allow to cool.

Preheat the oven to moderate
(160°C, 325°F, Gas Mark 3).
Roll out the pastry to line a
20-cm/8-inch loose-bottomed
flan tin. Bake blind for 15–20
minutes then allow to cool.
Spread the jam over the pastry
base and cover with the black-
berry mixture.

Whisk the egg whites until
stiff then whisk in half the
sugar and fold in the rest.
Pipe a lattice work over the
filling and bake in a moderate
oven (180°C, 350°F, Gas
Mark 4) for 15 minutes. Cool
before serving.

Fresh Plum Tart

PASTRY
300 g/10 oz plain flour
200 g/7 oz butter, cut into flakes
100 g/3½ oz castor sugar
1 egg
FILLING
1·5 kg/3 lb plums
2 tablespoons sugar crystals

Sift the flour into a mixing
bowl. Add the butter, sugar
and egg and mix well until a
dough is formed. Wrap in foil
or cling film and leave for
2 hours in the refrigerator.

Wash the plums, halve and
remove the stones and cut the
fruit into quarters. Preheat the
oven to moderately hot (200°C,
400°F, Gas Mark 6).

Roll out the pastry on a
floured surface and use to line a
25-cm/10-inch flan tin. Prick
the base of the flan all over
with a fork. Arrange the plums
in a rosette shape to fill the flan

and sprinkle sugar crystals over
the top. Bake the tart for 30–
35 minutes; cover with foil if
becoming too brown. Leave the
tart to cool on a wire rack,
sprinkle with extra sugar
crystals and serve with whipped
cream.

Favourites Baked with Fruit

Farmhouse Plum Flan

PASTRY
300 g/10 oz plain flour
200 g/7 oz butter, cut into flakes
100 g/3½ oz castor sugar
1 egg
FILLING AND DECORATION
1 kg/2 lb plums
100 g/4 oz sugar
20 g/¾ oz powdered gelatine
25 g/1 oz cornflour
2 tablespoons coarsely ground walnuts
150 ml/¼ pint double cream
12 walnut halves

Sift the flour into a mixing bowl. Add the butter, sugar and egg and mix well until a dough is formed. Wrap in foil or cling film and leave in the refrigerator for 2 hours.

Preheat the oven to moderately hot (200°C, 400°F, Gas Mark 6). Roll out the pastry on a floured surface to line a 25-cm/10-inch flan tin. Prick the base of the pastry case all over and bake blind for 20–25 minutes, until cooked. Leave to cool.

Wash and stone the plums and cook with 2 tablespoons water and the sugar for 10 minutes. Dissolve the gelatine in 3 tablespoons water over a gentle heat. Mix the cornflour with a little cold water, pour on to the plums and bring to the boil, stirring all the time. Stir in the walnuts. Mix the dissolved gelatine with the plum mixture and pour into the flan case. Leave to set in the refrigerator.

Whip the cream until stiff. Mark the flan into 12 portions and decorate with piped whipped cream and walnut halves.

Apricot Slice

YEAST DOUGH
225 g/8 oz plain flour
15 g/½ oz fresh yeast
5 tablespoons lukewarm milk
40 g/1½ oz butter
¼ beaten egg
pinch of salt
1 tablespoon castor sugar
TOPPING
675 g/1½ lb apricots or 2 (411-g/ 14¼-oz) cans apricot halves
350 g/12 oz curd or cottage cheese
2 eggs
15 g/½ oz cornflour
grated rind and juice of ½ lemon
40 g/1½ oz castor sugar
15 g/½ oz flaked almonds

Sift the flour into a mixing bowl. Cream the yeast with a little of the milk, then add the remaining milk. Make a well in the centre of the flour and pour in the yeast liquid. Sprinkle with a little flour from the edge of the bowl, cover and leave for 15 minutes, until frothy. Melt the butter and mix with the egg, salt and sugar. Pour into the flour, mixing well to form a dough. Knead the dough on a lightly floured board for 5 minutes, then cover and leave to rise for 30 minutes.

Wash, halve and stone the apricots, or drain if using canned fruit. Mix together the curd cheese or sieved cottage cheese, eggs, cornflour, lemon rind and juice and the sugar.

Grease a 33 × 23-cm/ 13 × 9-inch Swiss roll tin and roll out the yeast dough to fit it. Preheat the oven to hot (220°C, 425°F, Gas Mark 7).

Spread the cheese mixture over the dough base and arrange the apricots on top, cut side down. Sprinkle with the almonds and bake towards the top of the oven for 25–30 minutes. Leave to cool a little, cut into slices and remove from the tin.

Favourites Baked with Fruit

Blackcurrant Flan

PASTRY
200 g/7 oz plain flour
100 g/3¾ oz butter, cut into flakes
50 g/2 oz castor sugar
1 egg
2 tablespoons water
FILLING
500 g/1 lb blackcurrants
3 eggs, separated
125 g/4 oz castor sugar
125 g/4 oz ground almonds
icing sugar to sprinkle

Sift the flour into a mixing bowl. Add the butter, sugar, egg and water and mix until a dough is formed. Wrap the pastry in foil or cling film and leave in the refrigerator for 2 hours.

Remove the stalks from the blackcurrants, wash and dry on absorbent paper. Beat the egg yolks with half the sugar until frothy, then mix in the ground almonds. Whisk the egg whites until stiff, whisk in the remaining sugar then fold into the egg yolk mixture. Mix in the blackcurrants.

Preheat the oven to moderately hot (190°C, 375°F, Gas Mark 5). Roll out the pastry on a floured surface and use to line a 20-cm/8-inch flan tin. Prick the base lightly with a fork and spread the filling evenly over the pastry. Bake for 40 minutes. Leave to cool for 5 minutes in the tin, then transfer to a wire rack. Sift icing sugar over the top when it is completely cooled.

Cherry Cake

225 g/8 oz cherries
5 eggs, separated
180 g/7 oz castor sugar
80 g/3 oz butter or margarine, melted
180 g/7 oz plain flour
¼ teaspoon baking powder
icing sugar to sprinkle

Remove the stalks from the cherries, wash and stone the fruit and pat dry. Grease and flour a 23-cm/9-inch cake tin. Preheat the oven to moderately hot (190°C, 375°F, Gas Mark 5).

Beat the egg yolks with half the sugar until creamy, then whisk in the melted butter or margarine. Sift together the flour and baking powder and fold into the egg yolk mixture. Whisk the egg whites until stiff and add the rest of the sugar. Whisk again until stiff and fold into the yolk mixture. Turn into the cake tin and scatter the cherries over the top, pressing each one into the mixture with the handle of a wooden spoon. Bake for 50–60 minutes; during this time the cherries will sink into the mixture.

Turn the cake out of the tin, leave to cool on a wire rack and dust with sifted icing sugar.

Cook's Tip

Substitute 100 g/4 oz glacé cherries for the fresh cherries. Halve and toss in flour before adding to the cake.

Favourites Baked with Fruit

Rhubarb Meringue Tart

PASTRY
300 g/10 oz plain flour
200 g/7 oz butter or margarine,
  cut into flakes
100 g/3½ oz castor sugar
1 egg
TOPPING
1 kg/2 lb rhubarb
sugar to sprinkle
3 egg whites
150 g/5 oz castor sugar

Sift the flour into a mixing bowl. Add the butter, sugar and egg and mix until a dough is formed. Wrap the pastry in foil or cling film and leave for 2 hours in the refrigerator.

Wash the rhubarb, dry on absorbent paper and pull away the thin outer skin from the top downwards. Cut the sticks of rhubarb into 7·5-cm/3-inch lengths. Preheat the oven to moderately hot (200°C, 400°F, Gas Mark 6).

Roll out the pastry on a floured surface into a rectangle approximately 25 × 20 cm/ 10 × 8 inches. Carefully lift the pastry on to a baking tray and prick all over with a fork. Arrange the lengths of rhubarb next to one another on the pastry base and sprinkle with a little sugar to taste. Bake for 30 minutes then allow to cool slightly.

Whisk the egg whites until stiff, whisk in a little of the sugar then fold in the rest.

Put the meringue mixture into a piping bag fitted with a star nozzle and pipe an even, diagonal trellis over the top of the tart. Return to the oven and cook for a further 10 minutes, until the meringue is lightly browned.

Allow the tart to cool a little, cut into even slices and leave to cool on a wire rack.

Cook's Tip

If piping is too time-consuming, spread the meringue over the rhubarb with a palette knife. The tart won't look quite as distinguished, but it will taste just as good. You can also use blackberries, gooseberries or bilberries to make the flan.

Favourites Baked with Fruit

Dutch Apple Cake

PASTRY
300 g/11 oz plain flour
150 g/5½ oz butter, cut into
flakes
150 g/5½ oz castor sugar
2 egg yolks
pinch of salt
FILLING
500 g/1 lb cooking apples
75 g/3 oz castor sugar
juice of 1 lemon
pinch of ground cinnamon
50 g/2 oz raisins
50 g/2 oz ground almonds
50 g/2 oz ground hazelnuts
ICING
2 tablespoons apricot jam
50 g/2 oz icing sugar
2 tablespoons Kirsch or cherry
brandy

Sift the flour into a bowl. Rub
in the butter then stir in the
sugar, egg yolks and salt and
mix quickly to a dough. Wrap
in foil or cling film and leave
for 2 hours in the refrigerator.
Preheat the oven to moderately hot (200°C, 400°F, Gas
Mark 6). Roll out just over
half the pastry to line a 25-cm/
10-inch loose-bottomed flan tin
and bake blind for 15 minutes.
Peel, core and slice the
apples. Mix with the sugar,
lemon juice, cinnamon, raisins
and ground nuts. Moisten with
a little water to blend. Spoon
into the pastry case and smooth
over. Roll out the remaining
pastry to cover the filling and
seal the edges together well.
Bake for a further 30 minutes
then cool in the tin overnight.
Warm the jam and spread
over the top of the cake. Blend
the sifted icing sugar with the
Kirsch, spread over the jam
and leave to set.

Trellised Apple Flan

PASTRY
300 g/10 oz plain flour
200 g/7 oz butter, cut into flakes
100 g/3½ oz castor sugar
1 egg
grated rind of 1 lemon
FILLING
1 kg/2 lb cooking apples
juice of 1 lemon
50 g/2 oz raisins
50 g/2 oz castor sugar
¼ teaspoon ground cinnamon
2 eggs
3 tablespoons milk
1 tablespoon sugar
1 tablespoon custard powder

Sift the flour into a mixing
bowl. Add the butter, sugar,
egg and lemon rind and mix
until a dough is formed. Wrap
the pastry in foil or cling film
and leave for 2 hours in the
refrigerator.

Peel, core and slice the
apples and mix with the lemon
juice, raisins, castor sugar and
cinnamon. Preheat the oven to
moderately hot (200°C, 400°F,
Gas Mark 6).

Roll out the pastry and use
to line a 23-cm/9-inch loose-
bottomed flan tin. Keep back
some of the pastry for the
trellis and cut it into thin
strips. Prick the base of the flan
all over with a fork and arrange
the apple mixture on top.
Whisk together the eggs, milk,
sugar and custard powder and
pour over the apples. Arrange
the pastry strips on top in a
trellis pattern. Bake the flan
for 50–60 minutes, covering
with foil if it becomes too
brown.

Allow the flan to cool a little
in the tin then transfer to a
wire rack to cool completely.

Favourites Baked with Fruit

Alsace Apple Tart

PASTRY
200 g/7 oz plain flour
100 g/3¼ oz butter or margarine, cut into flakes
1 egg yolk
30 g/1 oz castor sugar
pinch of salt
2 tablespoons cold water
FILLING
1 kg/2 lb cooking apples
2 tablespoons lemon juice
100 g/4 oz castor sugar
3 eggs
125 ml/4 fl oz double cream
few drops of vanilla essence

Sift the flour into a mixing bowl. Add the butter, egg yolk, sugar, salt and water and mix until a dough is formed. Wrap in foil or cling film and leave for 2 hours in the refrigerator.

Peel the apples, quarter and remove the cores. Slice each apple quarter very thinly, keeping the quarter in shape, and sprinkle with the lemon juice. Preheat the oven to moderately hot (200°C, 400°F, Gas Mark 6).

Roll out the pastry to 5 mm/¼ inch thick and use to line a 23-cm/9-inch flan tin. Prick the base all over with a fork and arrange the sliced apple quarters on it. Bake for 20–25 minutes.

Meanwhile, beat the sugar with the eggs until frothy and add the cream and vanilla essence. Pour the egg mixture into the half-cooked flan and bake for a further 20–30 minutes.

Allow the flan to cool for a while in the tin then transfer to a wire rack to cool completely.

Apple Lattice Flan

PASTRY
450 g/1 lb plain flour
150 g/5 oz margarine, cut into flakes
25 g/1 oz castor sugar
½ teaspoon salt
150 ml/¼ pint water
FILLING
1 kg/2 lb cooking apples
grated rind and juice of 1 lemon
125 g/4½ oz sugar
1 teaspoon ground cinnamon
100 g/4 oz raisins
100 g/4 oz hazelnuts, chopped
GLAZE
1 egg yolk, beaten
4 tablespoons apricot jam
100 g/4 oz icing sugar
1½ tablespoons lemon juice

Sift the flour into a bowl and rub in the margarine. Add the sugar, salt and water and mix to a dough. Wrap in foil or cling film and leave for 1 hour in the refrigerator.

Peel the apples, chop roughly and mix with the lemon rind and juice, sugar, cinnamon, raisins and hazelnuts. Preheat the oven to moderately hot (200°C, 400°F, Gas Mark 6).

Roll out three-quarters of the pastry to line the base and sides of a 33 × 23-cm/13 × 9-inch Swiss roll tin. Spread the apple mixture over the pastry. Roll out the remaining pastry, cut into thin strips and arrange over the flan in a lattice pattern. Brush with beaten egg yolk and bake the flan for 30–40 minutes. Leave to cool.

Brush the pastry with the warmed apricot jam. Mix the sifted icing sugar and lemon juice together and use to glaze the trellis.

Favourites Baked with Fruit

Strawberry Ring

CHOUX PASTE
60 g/2 oz butter
pinch of salt
grated rind of ½ lemon
250 ml/8 fl oz water
200 g/7 oz plain flour
4 eggs, beaten
FILLING
500 g/1 lb strawberries
2 teaspoons vanilla sugar
450 ml/¾ pint double cream

First wash and hull the straw-berries. Reserve three large strawberries and mix the rest with the vanilla sugar; leave for a while for the sugar to be absorbed. Lightly grease a baking tray and dust with flour. Preheat the oven to hot (220°C, 425°F, Gas Mark 7).

Melt the butter with the salt, lemon rind and water over a low heat, then bring quickly to the boil. Remove from the heat, add the sifted flour, and beat with a wooden spoon until it comes away from the sides of the pan. Return to the heat for 1 minute, stirring continuously. Allow to cool slightly then add the eggs a little at a time, beating in well.

Fill a piping bag fitted with a large star nozzle with the mix-ture and pipe 11 rosette shapes in a 25-cm/10-inch ring on the baking tray. When risen they will join together to form a circle. Bake just below the centre for 20–25 minutes.

Purée the strawberries through a nylon sieve. Whip the cream until stiff and put 2 tablespoons of the cream into a clean piping bag fitted with a large star nozzle. Mix the remaining cream with the strawberry purée.

While still warm, split the choux ring to allow it to cool more quickly, then fill with the strawberry cream mixture. Decorate with rosettes of cream and segments of strawberry.

Strawberry Curd Cake

PASTRY
250 g/9 oz plain flour
125 g/4½ oz butter, cut into flakes
100 g/4 oz castor sugar
2 egg yolks
FILLING
225 g/8 oz curd cheese
100 g/4 oz castor sugar
1 tablespoon cornflour
grated rind of 1 lemon
4 eggs
450 ml/¾ pint double cream
225 g/8 oz strawberries
1 small packet quick-setting jel mix (red colour)

Knead together the sifted flour, butter, sugar and egg yolks. Wrap the pastry in foil or cling film and leave in the refrigera-tor for 2 hours.

Preheat the oven to moder-ately hot (200°C, 400°F, Gas Mark 6). Roll out the pastry on a lightly floured surface and use to line the base and sides of a 28-cm/11-inch springform cake tin. Prick thoroughly all over with a fork and bake blind for 10 minutes. Reduce the oven temperature to moderate (180°C, 350°F, Gas Mark 4).

Beat the curd cheese, sugar, cornflour, lemon rind and eggs together. Whip the cream until stiff and fold into the cheese mixture. Turn into the pastry case and bake for a further 50–60 minutes. Leave to cool slightly.

Wash and hull the straw-berries and dry on absorbent paper. Cut each strawberry in half and arrange over the curd cake. Prepare the jel mix according to the instructions on the packet and pour over the strawberries.

Favourites Baked with Fruit

Gooseberry Meringue Pie

PASTRY
250 g/9 oz plain flour
125 g/4½ oz butter, cut into flakes
25 g/1 oz castor sugar
1 egg
FILLING
500 g/1 lb gooseberries
450 ml/¾ pint water
25 g/1 oz granulated sugar
25 g/1 oz castor sugar
450 ml/¾ pint milk
2 egg yolks
20 g/¾ oz cornflour
MERINGUE
3 egg whites
150 g/5 oz icing sugar

Sift the flour into a bowl. Add the butter, sugar and egg and mix to a dough. Wrap in foil or cling film and chill for 2 hours.

Wash the gooseberries and top and tail them. Cook in the water with the granulated sugar for 15 minutes and allow to cool in a sieve over a basin. Preheat the oven to moderately hot (200°C, 400°F, Gas Mark 6).

Roll out the pastry to line the base and sides of a 23-cm/9-inch sandwich cake tin. Prick all over with a fork and bake blind for 20 minutes.

Meanwhile, whisk the castor sugar with 3 tablespoons milk, the egg yolks and cornflour. Bring the rest of the milk to the boil, pour on to the cornflour mixture then return to the saucepan. Bring to the boil, stirring until thickened. Pour into the pastry case and arrange the gooseberries on top.

Whisk the egg whites until very stiff then add the sifted icing sugar and whisk again. Spread this meringue over the gooseberries and cook for 5–10 minutes in a hot oven (220°C, 425°F, Gas Mark 7).

Raspberry Meringue Nest

MERINGUE
6 egg whites
175 g/6 oz castor sugar
150 g/5 oz icing sugar
30 g/1 oz cornflour
FILLING
250 ml/8 fl oz double cream
1 tablespoon brandy
350 g/12 oz raspberries

Line a baking tray with non-stick baking parchment. Preheat the oven to very cool (110°C, 225°F, Gas Mark ¼).

Whisk the egg whites until stiff then gradually whisk in the castor sugar. Fold in the sifted icing sugar and cornflour. Fill a piping bag fitted with a large plain nozzle with the mixture, and pipe in a spiral on to the baking tray to make a 20–23-cm/8–9-inch round base. Form the sides of the meringue nest by piping individual rosettes over the edge. Allow to dry out in the oven for 12 hours, leaving the oven door slightly ajar.

Remove from the oven and leave to cool. Whip the cream with the brandy until thick. Spread this cream into the meringue nest and cover with the raspberries.

Cook's Tip

To make Gooseberry Meringue Nests, as illustrated on the jacket, pipe 7·5-cm/3-inch nests using a small star nozzle. Fill with whipped cream and drained canned gooseberries.

French Orange Flan

PASTRY
100 g/4 oz butter
50 g/2 oz icing sugar
1 egg yolk
150 g/6 oz plain flour
FILLING
4 tablespoons orange jelly
   marmalade
250 ml/8 fl oz double cream
100 g/4 oz castor sugar
6 eggs
grated rind of 3 lemons
DECORATION
1 orange
50 g/2 oz sugar
2 tablespoons water
4 cherries

Knead together the butter, sifted icing sugar and egg yolk. Sift the flour on to this mixture and work in quickly with the fingertips. Cover the dough and leave for 2 hours in the refrigerator.

Preheat the oven to moderately hot (200°C, 400°F, Gas Mark 6). Roll out the pastry to a thickness of about 3 mm/⅛ inch and carefully line two 15-cm/6-inch flan dishes. Spread the base of the flans with the orange marmalade. Beat the cream, sugar, eggs and lemon rind together until frothy and pour into the flan cases. Cook for 45–50 minutes.

Peel the orange carefully, removing all the pith, and slice thinly. Dissolve the sugar in the water over a low heat, stirring continuously until the sugar has completely dissolved. Place the orange slices in the hot sugar syrup, leave for 3 minutes and then drain. Arrange over the flans and top with the cherries, also glazed in the sugar syrup.

Chinese Gooseberry Cream Tart

1 (368-g/13-oz) packet frozen
   puff pastry, thawed
1 egg yolk, beaten to glaze
FILLING
250 ml/8 fl oz double cream
2 tablespoons castor sugar
1½ teaspoons powdered gelatine
1 tablespoon rum
6 Chinese gooseberries
1½ teaspoons arrowroot

Roll out the pastry quite thinly and cut out a 20-cm/8-inch round from the centre. Using a 5-cm/2-inch round cutter, cut out 12 half-moon shapes from the surrounding pastry. Sprinkle a baking tray with cold water, place the pastry round on it and brush with beaten egg yolk. Prick the pastry all over with a fork.

Place the half-moon shapes around the edge of the pastry and brush these with egg yolk. Leave in the refrigerator for 15 minutes. Preheat the oven to hot (220°C, 425°F, Gas Mark 7) and bake towards the top of the oven for 15 minutes. Cool on a wire rack.

Whip the cream and sugar together until stiff. Dissolve the gelatine in 3 tablespoons hot water over a gentle heat. Allow to cool then stir into the cream with the rum. When half-set, spread the cream over the pastry base, mounding it up in the centre, and leave in the refrigerator until firm.

Peel the Chinese gooseberries, cut into slices and arrange overlapping on the cream. Blend the arrowroot in a pan with a little water. Add 150 ml/¼ pint cold water and bring to the boil, stirring continuously. Leave until just warm then pour over the fruit to glaze.

Exotic Fruit Gâteaux

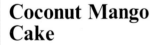

Coconut Mango Cake

SPONGE MIXTURE
2 eggs, separated, plus 2 egg
*   yolks*
50 g/2 oz castor sugar
40 g/1½ oz plain flour
15 g/½ oz cornflour
20 g/¾ oz cocoa powder
FILLING AND TOPPING
2 mangoes or 2 (415-g/15-oz)
*   cans*
3 tablespoons white wine
2 egg yolks
100 g/4 oz castor sugar
15 g/½ oz powdered gelatine
450 ml/¾ pint double cream
1 tablespoon icing sugar
50 g/2 oz long-thread coconut

Grease and flour a 23-cm/9-inch cake tin. Preheat the oven to hot (220°C, 425°F, Gas Mark 7).

Beat all the egg yolks with half the sugar until pale and creamy. Whisk the egg whites until stiff and fold in the remaining sugar. Carefully fold into the egg yolk mixture. Sift the flour, cornflour and cocoa powder together then carefully fold into the eggs. Pour into the cake tin and bake for about 15 minutes. Cool on a wire rack then slice into two layers.

Peel or drain the mangoes and dice. Mix the wine, egg yolks and castor sugar in a basin over hot water. Cook until thick, stirring, but do not boil. Remove from the heat. Dissolve the gelatine in 3 tablespoons water over a gentle heat. Stir into the wine mixture with most of the diced mango and allow to cool. Whip the cream. Fold half into the wine mixture and use to sandwich the cake layers together. Leave until set. Mix the remaining cream with the icing sugar and spread over the top and sides. Sprinkle with the coconut and decorate as illustrated.

Tropical Fruit Gâteau

PASTRY
125 g/4 oz plain flour
60 g/2 oz butter
45 g/1½ oz icing sugar
pinch of salt
1 egg yolk
FILLING
2 tablespoons apricot jam
1 (20-cm/8-inch) sandwich cake
*   (see page 228)*
1 (44-g/1½-oz) packet dessert
*   topping mix*
150 ml/¼ pint milk
TOPPING
4 pineapple rings
2 Chinese gooseberries
1 mango
5 cocktail cherries
2 tablespoons pineapple juice
50 g/2 oz toasted flaked almonds

Sift the flour into a bowl and knead in the butter, sifted icing sugar, salt and egg yolk. Cover the pastry dough and leave for 2 hours in the refrigerator.

Preheat the oven to hot (220°C, 425°F, Gas Mark 7). Roll out the pastry to line the base of a 20-cm/8-inch loose-bottomed flan tin and bake for 20–30 minutes.

Leave to cool then remove from the tin and brush with the warmed jam. Place the cake on top of the pastry base. Make up the dessert topping with the milk, according to the instructions on the packet, and spread over the top and sides of the gâteau.

Cut the pineapple rings into pieces. Peel the Chinese gooseberries and mango and slice. Halve the cherries. Arrange the fruit over the gâteau and sprinkle with the pineapple juice. Press toasted flaked almonds on to the sides of the gâteau.

Sweet Pecan Nut Pie

PASTRY
180 g/6 oz butter, cut into flakes
pinch of salt
4 tablespoons iced water
250 g/9 oz plain flour
FILLING
3 eggs
100 g/4 oz black treacle
50 g/2 oz golden syrup
40 g/1½ oz plain flour
60 g/2 oz butter
¼ teaspoon vanilla essence
pinch of salt
250 g/9 oz pecan nuts, halved

Knead the butter, salt and iced water into the sifted flour. Wrap the pastry in foil or cling film and leave for 2 hours in the refrigerator.

Preheat the oven to moderately hot (200°C, 400°F, Gas Mark 6). Roll out the pastry to line the base and sides of a 25-cm/10-inch loose-bottomed flan tin. Do not prick the base with a fork. Bake blind for 10–12 minutes.

Meanwhile, beat the eggs lightly, add the treacle and syrup and beat in well to mix. Stir in the flour and melted, slightly cooled butter. Lastly fold in the vanilla, salt and nuts. Pour this filling into the pastry case and bake the pie for a further 25–30 minutes.

Cook's Tip
Instead of pecan nuts, try making this pie with walnuts or brazil nuts.

Chocolate Almond Roll

5 eggs, separated
180 g/6 oz castor sugar
pinch of salt
pinch of ground cinnamon
¼ teaspoon vanilla essence
grated rind of ¼ lemon
50 g/2 oz butter
90 g/3½ oz plain chocolate, grated
100 g/4 oz plain flour
100 g/4 oz ground almonds
ICING
100 g/4 oz plain chocolate
50 g/2 oz toasted flaked almonds

Grease a Balmoral tin or 1-kg/2-lb·loaf tin and sprinkle with fine breadcrumbs. Preheat the oven to moderately hot (190°C, 375°F, Gas Mark 5).

Whisk the egg yolks with half the sugar, the salt, cinnamon, vanilla essence and lemon rind, until pale and creamy.

Melt the butter and leave to cool slightly. Whisk the egg whites until stiff and fold in the remaining sugar. Fold a quarter of these egg whites into the egg yolk mixture, then fold in the grated chocolate, sifted flour, ground almonds and remaining egg white. Lastly fold in the melted butter. Turn into the prepared tin, smooth the surface and bake for 40–50 minutes.

Allow the cake to cool on a wire rack. Melt the chocolate in a basin over hot water and spread over the roll. Sprinkle with flaked almonds and leave to set.

Daisy Cake

300 g/12 oz butter
100 g/4 oz ground almonds
6 eggs, separated
grated rind of 1 lemon
few drops of vanilla essence
140 g/5 oz castor sugar
120 g/4½ oz plain flour
80 g/3 oz cornflour
ICING
150 g/5 oz apricot jam
200 g/7 oz icing sugar
1 tablespoon lemon juice
1 tablespoon water

Grease a 23-cm/9-inch round
fluted cake tin and sprinkle
with fine breadcrumbs. Preheat
the oven to moderately hot
(190°C, 375°F, Gas Mark 5).

Cream the softened butter
with the ground almonds. Stir
in the egg yolks, lemon rind
and vanilla essence. Whisk the
egg whites until stiff then carefully fold in the sugar. Fold the
egg whites into the butter mixture. Sift the flour and cornflour together and fold into the
mixture. Turn into the prepared
cake tin, smooth the surface
and bake for 50–60 minutes.

Leave to cool slightly on a
wire rack, then spread with the
warmed apricot jam. Leave to
cool and set for 30 minutes.
Mix the sifted icing sugar with
the lemon juice and water and
spread over the cake.

Hazelnut Loaf Cake

250 g/9 oz soft margarine
200 g/7 oz castor sugar
25 g/1 oz vanilla sugar
4 eggs
250 g/9 oz ground hazelnuts
250 g/9 oz self-raising flour
1 teaspoon baking powder
1 tablespoon brandy
icing sugar to sprinkle

Grease a 1-kg/2-lb loaf tin. Preheat the oven to moderate (180°C, 350°F, Gas Mark 4).
   Cream the margarine, sugar and vanilla sugar until light and fluffy. Stir in the eggs, one at a time, then the hazelnuts. Sift the flour and baking powder together and fold into the mixture, making sure all is thoroughly mixed. Finally stir in the brandy. Turn into the tin and bake for 1–1¼ hours.
   Allow the cake to cool on a wire rack, then sprinkle with sifted icing sugar.

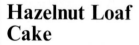

Cook's Tip

For deeper cakes, test the cooking with a warmed metal skewer. Towards the end of cooking time, insert the warmed skewer into the middle of the cake and then withdraw; if it comes out clean then the cake is cooked.

Crumble Cake

200 g/7 oz soft margarine
200 g/7 oz castor sugar
1 egg
grated rind of 1 lemon
500 g/1 lb 2 oz plain flour
1 teaspoon baking powder
1 (454-g/1-lb) jar cherry jam
50 g/2 oz ground almonds
icing sugar to sprinkle

Grease a 25-cm/10-inch spring-form cake tin with margarine. Preheat the oven to hot (220°C, 425°F, Gas Mark 7).
   Beat the margarine and sugar together until creamy. Stir in the egg and lemon rind. Sift the flour and baking powder and fold a few tablespoons into the creamed mixture. Tip the remaining flour on to the mixture and, with the fingertips, work quickly into crumbs. Place half this crumb mixture in the prepared cake tin and spread with the jam. Mix the rest with the almonds and crumble over the jam. Bake the cake for 50–60 minutes.
   Leave to cool on a wire rack and dust with sifted icing sugar.

Iced Orange Loaf Cake

250 g/9 oz soft margarine
250 g/9 oz castor sugar
3 eggs plus 4 egg yolks
100 g/4 oz self-raising flour
pinch of salt
1 tablespoon orange liqueur
grated rind of 2 oranges
grated rind of 1 lemon
2 tablespoons orange juice
1 tablespoon lemon juice
100 g/4 oz cornflour
100 g/4 oz ground almonds
75 g/3 oz candied orange peel,
    finely chopped
ICING
50 g/2 oz orange jelly
    marmalade
200 g/7 oz icing sugar
2 tablespoons orange juice
25 g/1 oz candied orange peel,
    finely chopped

Grease a 1-kg/2-lb loaf tin and
sprinkle with fine breadcrumbs.

Preheat the oven to moderate
(180°C, 350°F, Gas Mark 4).
    Cream the margarine and
sugar together until light and
fluffy. Stir in the eggs and egg
yolks, one by one, along with a
few tablespoons of the flour.
Mix in the salt, liqueur, fruit
rinds and juice. Sift the remaining flour with the cornflour and
fold into the cake mixture with
the ground almonds and
candied peel. Turn into the tin
and bake for about 1¼ hours.
    Cool on a wire rack then
spread the top of the cake with
the warmed orange jelly. Mix
together the sifted icing sugar
and orange juice and spread
over the cake. Sprinkle with
the candied peel to decorate.

Marzipan Cake

MARZIPAN
120 g/4½ oz almond paste
100 g/4 oz pistachio nuts or
    blanched almonds, grated
1 tablespoon arrack or ouzo
CAKE MIXTURE
250 g/9 oz soft margarine
240 g/8¼ oz castor sugar
5 eggs, separated
pinch of salt
1 tablespoon arrack or ouzo
few drops of vanilla essence
230 g/8 oz plain flour
85 g/3 oz cornflour
1 teaspoon baking powder
ICING
175 g/6 oz plain chocolate
25 g/1 oz pistachio nuts, chopped

Grease a 20–23-cm/8–9-inch
round fluted cake tin and
sprinkle with fine breadcrumbs.
Preheat the oven to moderately hot (190°C, 375°F, Gas
Mark 5).
    Knead the almond paste with

the pistachios and arrack, roll
out to a thickness of 1 cm/
½ inch and cut into 1-cm/½-inch
cubes.
    Beat the margarine with half
the sugar, the egg yolks, salt,
arrack and vanilla essence until
well mixed. Whisk the egg
whites until stiff and whisk in
the remaining sugar. Fold into
the egg yolk mixture. Sift together the flour, cornflour and
baking powder and mix in the
marzipan cubes. Fold all this
thoroughly into the egg mixture. Turn into the cake tin and
bake for 1¼–1½ hours. Turn
out and cool on a wire rack.
    Melt the chocolate in a basin
over hot water and spread over
the cake. Decorate with the
chopped pistachios while still
soft and leave the icing to set.

Fresh Strawberry Savarin

SAVARIN DOUGH
20 g/¾ oz fresh yeast
250 ml/8 fl oz lukewarm milk
350 g/12 oz plain flour
4 eggs
40 g/1½ oz castor sugar
1 tablespoon vanilla sugar
¼ teaspoon salt
150 g/5 oz butter or margarine
SYRUP
4 tablespoons rum
6 tablespoons white wine
250 ml/8 fl oz water
150 g/5 oz sugar
FILLING
225 g/8 oz strawberries
150 ml/¼ pint double cream
50 g/2 oz castor sugar
1 teaspoon chopped pistachio
    nuts

Grease a 23-cm/9-inch savarin tin and dust with flour.

Cream the yeast with a little of the milk, then add the remaining milk. Sift the flour into a bowl, make a well in the centre and pour in the yeast liquid. Sprinkle with a little of the flour, cover and leave for 15 minutes, until frothy.

Beat the eggs with the sugar until frothy, then mix in the vanilla sugar, salt and melted butter. Add this to the yeast mixture, beating well to an almost pouring consistency. Cover and leave to rise for 10 minutes. Beat the mixture with a wooden spoon and pour into the savarin tin. Cover and leave until the mixture almost reaches the top of the tin.

Preheat the oven to hot (220°C, 425°F, Gas Mark 7). Bake the savarin for 40 minutes then turn out on to a wire rack.

Heat the rum, white wine, water and sugar until the sugar has dissolved. Simmer for 5 minutes. Place a container underneath the wire rack to catch the syrup then pour it over the savarin until completely absorbed. Place on to a serving plate.

Wash, hull and halve the strawberries. Whip the cream with the sugar until stiff. Place most of the strawberries in the centre of the savarin and pipe the cream over them. Use the remaining strawberries and pistachios to decorate.

Cook's Tip

This well known French sweet can also be served in the following classic ways.
Savarin Chantilly The savarin is steeped in sugar syrup and Kirsch, brushed with an apricot glaze and filled with whipped cream.
Savarin with Raspberries (aux Framboises). The savarin is steeped in sugar syrup and raspberry liqueur then filled with whipped cream and raspberries.

Marzipan Twist

YEAST DOUGH
20 g/¾ oz fresh yeast
6 tablespoons lukewarm milk
350 g/12 oz plain flour
50 g/2 oz butter
1 egg, beaten
50 g/2 oz castor sugar
pinch of salt
grated rind of ½ lemon
FILLING
225 g/8 oz ground almonds
2 egg whites
50 g/2 oz castor sugar
2 tablespoons rum
GLAZE
3 tablespoons icing sugar
1 tablespoon lemon juice
2 tablespoons water

Cream the yeast with a little of
the milk, then mix in the
remaining milk. Sift the flour
into a bowl, make a well in the
centre and pour in the yeast
liquid. Sprinkle a little flour
over the yeast, cover and leave

for 15 minutes, until frothy.
Melt the butter and mix with
the egg sugar, salt and lemon
rind. Stir into the yeast mixture
and mix all together to a
dough. Knead on a lightly
floured board until smooth.
Cover and leave to rise for
30–40 minutes.
Mix the ground almonds
with the egg whites, sugar and
rum. Roll out the yeast dough
to an oblong 45 × 30 cm/
18 × 12 inches, spread with the
almond filling, and roll up
lengthways. Cut the roll into
two equal lengths and twist the
two pieces around each other
to make a single plait. Place on
a greased baking tray and leave
to rise for 15 minutes.
Preheat the oven to moderately hot (200°C, 400°F, Gas
Mark 6) and bake for 35
minutes. Mix the sifted icing
sugar with lemon juice and
water and use to glaze the twist
while still warm.

Surprise Almond Plait

YEAST DOUGH
350 g/12 oz plain flour
20 g/¾ oz fresh yeast
6 tablespoons lukewarm milk
50 g/2 oz butter, melted
2 eggs
50 g/2 oz castor sugar
½ teaspoon salt
FILLING
50 g/2 oz ground almonds
4 tablespoons apricot jam
50 g/2 oz raisins
50 g/2 oz almonds, chopped
GLAZE
1 egg yolk, beaten
1 tablespoon sugar
1 tablespoon water

Sift the flour into a bowl and
make a well. Cream the yeast
with the milk and pour into the
flour well. Cover and leave for
15 minutes, until frothy. Mix
the butter with the eggs, sugar

and salt. Pour into the yeast
liquid and work with the flour
to form a dough. Knead for 5
minutes, cover and leave to
rise for 30–40 minutes. Roll
out to a 45 × 30-cm/18 × 12-
inch rectangle, and mark into
three equal strips lengthways.
Mix the ground almonds
with the jam and spread over
the middle strip. Sprinkle with
the raisins and almonds. Cut
the two outside strips into 1·5-
cm/¾-inch wide slanting strips
and plait together over the
filling. Place on a greased
baking tray, cover and leave to
rise for 15 minutes.
Preheat the oven to hot
(220°C, 425°F, Gas Mark 7).
Brush the plait with beaten egg
yolk and bake for 10 minutes.
Reduce to 190°C, 375°F, Gas
Mark 5 and bake for a further
10–12 minutes. Brush with a
sugar and water glaze.

Cakes for Morning Coffee

Berlin Speciality Cake

300 g/11 oz plain flour
15 g/½ oz fresh yeast
5 tablespoons lukewarm milk
100 g/4 oz castor sugar
175 g/6 oz butter
pinch of salt
3 eggs
grated rind of 1 lemon
200 g/7 oz currants
ICING
100–150 g/4–6 oz plain
  chocolate
1 tablespoon pine nuts

Grease a 20–23-cm/8–9-inch kugelhopf tin and sprinkle with fine breadcrumbs.

Sift the flour into a bowl and make a well in the centre. Cream the yeast with the milk and a little of the sugar. Pour into the well and sprinkle over a little flour. Cover and leave for 15 minutes, until frothy.

Melt the butter and combine with the remaining sugar, the salt, eggs and lemon rind. Pour into the well in the flour, mix all together and beat the dough until it bubbles. Cover and leave to rise for 30–40 minutes.

Preheat the oven to moderate (180°C, 350°F, Gas Mark 4). Wash and dry the currants and knead into the dough. Turn into the prepared tin and bake for 50–60 minutes.

Turn the cake out on to a wire rack and leave to cool. Melt the chocolate in a basin over hot water and pour over the cake to cover it completely. Sprinkle with the pine nuts while the icing is still soft.

Viennese Kugelhopf

500 g/1 lb 2 oz plain flour
25 g/1 oz fresh yeast
7 tablespoons lukewarm milk
150 g/5 oz castor sugar
150 g/5 oz butter
5 eggs, separated
pinch of salt
6 tablespoons single cream
75 g/3 oz sultanas
2 tablespoons rum
grated rind of 1 lemon
icing sugar to sprinkle

The Viennese kugelhopf is particularly small; if possible bake the given quantity of dough in three 16-cm/6½-inch kugelhopf tins. To bake the slightly larger kugelhopfs, illustrated on the jacket, use two 20-cm/8-inch tins. Grease the tins.

Sift the flour into a mixing bowl and make a well in the centre. Cream the yeast with the milk and a little of the sugar. Pour into the well and sprinkle over a little flour. Cover and leave for 15 minutes, until frothy.

Melt the butter and whisk with the remaining sugar, the egg yolks, salt and cream until frothy. Stir into the yeast mixture with the sultanas, rum and lemon rind and work in the rest of the flour. Whisk the egg whites until stiff, fold them into the dough and beat the mixture until it bubbles. Turn into the prepared tins, filling each one two-thirds full. Leave to rise for 15 minutes.

Preheat the oven to moderately hot (200°C, 400°F, Gas Mark 6) and bake for 40–60 minutes. Turn out on to a wire rack and sift with icing sugar when cool.

Poppy Seed Garland

YEAST DOUGH
500 g/1 lb 2 oz plain flour
40 g/1½ oz fresh yeast
100 g/4 oz castor sugar
250 ml/8 fl oz lukewarm milk
125 g/4½ oz butter
2 eggs
grated rind and juice of 1 lemon
pinch of salt
1 egg yolk, beaten
FILLING
2 teaspoons poppy seeds
1 tablespoon hot water
175 g/6 oz raisins
pinch of salt
pinch of ground cinnamon
ICING
3 tablespoons icing sugar
1 teaspoon lemon juice
1 tablespoon water
4 glacé cherries

Grease a 23-cm/9-inch ring tin with butter or margarine.

Sift the flour into a bowl and form a well in the centre. Cream the yeast with 1 teaspoon of the sugar, the milk and a little of the flour. Pour into the well and leave for 15 minutes, until frothy.

Melt the butter and add to the yeast mixture with the remaining sugar, the eggs, lemon rind and juice, and salt. Mix to a smooth dough with the rest of the flour and beat until the mixture comes away from the sides of the bowl. Cover the dough and leave to rise for 20 minutes.

Put the poppy seeds in a bowl, cover with the hot water and leave to soak for 5 minutes. Wash the raisins in hot water, dry well on absorbent paper and chop finely. Carefully drain the poppy seeds and mix in the chopped raisins, salt and cinnamon.

Preheat the oven to moder-

ately hot (200°C, 400°F, Gas Mark 6). Roll the dough out to a 50 × 25-cm/20 × 10-inch rectangle on a floured surface. Sprinkle the poppy seed mixture over the top and roll up the dough from the longest edge, making sure the ends are as thick as the centre. Brush the edges and ends with beaten egg yolk and press to seal. Place the roll in the ring tin with the seam on top and press the ends together firmly so the filling does not escape. Bake for 50–60 minutes.

Turn the cake out on to a wire rack to cool. Mix together the sifted icing sugar, lemon juice and water and use to ice the cake, then decorate with halved glacé cherries.

Cook's Tip
Yeast mixtures rise more quickly in a warm room temperature. However, if more convenient the dough may be covered and left overnight in the refrigerator to rise. The following day the dough should be returned to room temperature for about 1 hour before proceeding.

Pear Cheesecake

PASTRY
125 g/4 oz plain flour
60 g/2 oz butter, cut into flakes
45 g/1¼ oz icing sugar
¼ teaspoon vanilla sugar
pinch of salt
1 egg yolk
FILLING
1 (410-g/14½-oz) can pear halves
3 tablespoons Kirsch
250 g/9 oz curd or cream cheese
125 g/4½ oz castor sugar
juice of 1 lemon
20 g/¾ oz powdered gelatine
TOPPING
250 ml/8 fl oz double cream
25 g/1 oz castor sugar
3 tablespoons crushed praline (see page 231)
4 tablespoons redcurrant jelly

Sift the flour into a bowl. Add the butter, icing sugar, vanilla sugar, salt and egg yolk and mix to a dough. Cover and chill in the refrigerator for 2 hours.

Preheat the oven to moderately hot (200°C, 400°F, Gas Mark 6). Roll out the pastry to line a 20-cm/8-inch loose-bottomed flan tin and bake blind for 30 minutes. Cool.

Drain the pears and reserve the juice. Moisten the pears with a little Kirsch. Beat the cheese, sugar, lemon juice and remaining Kirsch together. Dissolve the gelatine in 3 tablespoons of the pear juice over a gentle heat. Stir into the cheese mixture. Arrange the pears in the pastry case, spread over the cheese mixture and leave to set.

Whip the cream with the sugar until stiff. Mix two-thirds of the cream with 2 tablespoons of the crushed praline and half the redcurrant jelly. Spread over the cheesecake. Decorate with rosettes of the remaining cream, redcurrant jelly and crushed praline.

Grape Cheesecake

SPONGE MIXTURE
4 eggs, separated
2 tablespoons lukewarm water
140 g/5 oz castor sugar
120 g/4 oz plain flour
60 g/2 oz cornflour
1 teaspoon baking powder
FILLING
450 g/1 lb curd or cream cheese
2 egg yolks
150 g/5 oz castor sugar
juice of 1 lemon
20 g/¾ oz powdered gelatine
250 ml/8 fl oz double cream
TOPPING
100 g/4 oz green grapes
225 g/8 oz black grapes
1 small packet quick-setting jel mix
100 g/4 oz toasted flaked almonds

Grease the base of a 23-cm/9-inch springform cake tin.

Preheat the oven to moderately hot (190°C, 375°F, Gas Mark 5).

Whisk the egg yolks with the water and half the sugar until frothy. Whisk the whites until stiff then fold in the remaining sugar. Fold into the egg yolks. Sift the flour with the cornflour and baking powder and fold in. Turn into the cake tin and bake for 40 minutes. Cool on a wire rack for 2 hours.

Beat the cheese with the egg yolks, sugar and lemon juice. Dissolve the gelatine in 3 tablespoons water over a gentle heat. Whip the cream until thick and fold into the cheese mixture with the cooled gelatine. Cut the sponge into two layers, sandwich thickly together with the cheese mixture, spreading the rest over the top and sides of the cake. Arrange the grapes on top, as illustrated. Glaze with the jel mix and finally press the flaked almonds on to the sides.

Rich Cream Cheesecake

SHORTBREAD
200 g/7 oz plain flour
120 g/4 oz butter, cut into flakes
70 g/2¼ oz castor sugar
1 egg yolk
pinch of salt
grated rind of ½ lemon
FILLING
250 ml/8 fl oz milk
200 g/7 oz castor sugar
pinch of salt
grated rind of 1 lemon
4 egg yolks
25 g/1 oz powdered gelatine
450 ml/¾ pint double cream
450 g/1 lb curd or cream cheese
icing sugar to sprinkle

Sift the flour on to a large board and dot with the flaked butter. Make a well in the centre, add the sugar, egg yolk, salt and lemon rind. Working from the centre outwards, quickly knead all the ingredients to a smooth dough. Shape into a ball, wrap in foil or cling film and leave for 2 hours in the refrigerator.

Preheat the oven to moderately hot (190°C, 375°F, Gas Mark 5). Roll the shortbread out thinly on a floured surface to make two 25-cm/10-inch rounds. Place on greased baking trays and bake for 8–10 minutes, until golden brown. While still warm, cut one round into 12 equal portions and cool on wire rack with the other round.

Place the milk, sugar, salt, lemon rind and egg yolks in the top of a double saucepan or in a basin over a pan of hot water. Heat gently, stirring continuously until smooth and thickened. Remove from the heat. Dissolve the gelatine in 3 tablespoons water over a gentle heat. Stir into the custard and leave to cool. Whip the cream until thick. When the custard begins to set, stir in the beaten cream cheese then carefully fold in the whipped cream.

Line the sides of a 25-cm/10-inch springform cake tin with a strip of greaseproof paper. Place the uncut shortbread round in the base of the tin, spoon over the cheese filling and smooth the surface. Arrange the cut shortbread on top to form a complete round then allow to set in the refrigerator.

Remove the cheesecake from the tin and carefully peel away the greaseproof paper. Finally sprinkle with sifted icing sugar.

Cook's Tip

If wished, fresh or frozen strawberries, raspberries, redcurrants or blackcurrants can be added to the cheese mixture. Make sure the frozen fruit has thawed sufficiently and is drained and sweetened to taste. If fresh fruit is used, wash, pat dry and sprinkle with sugar. Leave for a few minutes before adding to the mixture.

Pineapple Cream Gâteau

SPONGE MIXTURE
6 eggs, separated
150 g/5 oz castor sugar
100 g/4 oz plain flour
50 g/2 oz cornflour
50 g/2 oz cocoa powder
50 g/2 oz ground almonds
50 g/2 oz butter
FILLING AND TOPPING
25 g/1 oz cornflour
160 g/5½ oz castor sugar
500 ml/17 fl oz milk
250 g/9 oz butter
1 tablespoon rum
7 slices canned pineapple
80 g/3 oz toasted flaked almonds
7 glacé cherries

Grease the base and sides of a 25-cm/10-inch springform cake tin. Preheat the oven to moderately hot (190°C, 375°F, Gas Mark 5).

Whisk the egg yolks with a third of the sugar until thick and creamy. Whisk the egg whites until stiff, gradually add the remaining sugar and fold in well. Sift the flour with the cornflour and cocoa powder and mix in the ground almonds. Fold the egg whites into the egg yolks and then carefully fold in the flour mixture. Melt the butter, cool slightly and stir into the mixture. Turn into the prepared tin and bake for 35–45 minutes. Cool for a few minutes in the tin then remove to a wire rack for at least 2 hours.

Blend the cornflour and sugar with a little of the milk. Heat the remaining milk and pour on to the blended cornflour. Return to the saucepan and bring to the boil, stirring continuously. Cook for a few minutes to thicken then allow to cool, stirring frequently. Beat the butter until pale and creamy then beat in the rum. When the sauce is sufficiently cooled, add it gradually to the butter, beating each addition in well.

Cut the cake through twice, to make three layers. Cut the pineapple slices into small cubes and reserve 14 for decoration. Spread the bottom cake layer with butter cream, arrange the pineapple cubes on top and cover with a little more of the cream. Place the second cake layer over this, spread with butter cream and top with the last cake layer. Spread the top and sides of the cake thinly with the cream and put the remainder into a piping bag. Cover the gâteau with toasted flaked almonds, pipe 14 rosettes of cream around the top and place a pineapple cube and halved glacé cherry on each.

Cook's Tip

When whisking egg yolks and sugar together for a sponge it is quicker to use an electric mixer. If you do not have an electric mixer, stand the bowl over a pan of hot water and use a rotary or balloon whisk. The mixture is ready when the whisk leaves a trail.

Gooseberry Meringue Gâteau

SPONGE MIXTURE
6 eggs, separated
150 g/5 oz castor sugar
120 g/4 oz plain flour
60 g/2 oz cornflour
50 g/2 oz ground almonds
50 g/2 oz butter
FILLING
150 g/5 oz ground almonds
3 tablespoons rum
2 tablespoons icing sugar
3 tablespoons water
TOPPING
500 g/1 lb gooseberries
3 tablespoons granulated sugar
6 tablespoons water
4 egg whites
170 g/6 oz castor sugar
few drops'of vanilla essence
100 g/4 oz toasted flaked
  almonds

Grease the base and sides of a 25-cm/10-inch springform cake tin. Preheat the oven to moderately hot (190°C, 375°F, Gas Mark 5).

Whisk the egg yolks with a third of the sugar until creamy. Whisk the egg whites until stiff, then gradually fold in the rest of the sugar. Sift the flour with the cornflour and mix with the ground almonds. Fold the egg whites into the egg yolks then fold in the flour mixture. Melt the butter, cool slightly and stir into the mixture. Turn into the prepared tin and bake for 35–40 minutes. Cool on a wire rack for at least 2 hours then slice through into two layers.

Mix the ground almonds with the rum, icing sugar and water to form a smooth paste. Use to sandwich the cake layers together.

Top, tail and wash the gooseberries. Mix the granulated sugar with the water, bring to the boil, add the gooseberries

and simmer over a gentle heat for 10 minutes. Drain thoroughly in a sieve over a basin.

Preheat the oven to hot (230°C, 450°F, Gas Mark 8). Whisk the egg whites until stiff, then whisk in the sugar and fold in the vanilla essence. Arrange the gooseberries over the cake, reserving 14 whole gooseberries for decoration. Spread the meringue mixture thickly over the top and sides. Pipe 14 meringue garlands on top, working from the centre outwards and ending each in a rosette. Bake the cake for 1 minute only until the meringue is light golden brown on top. Decorate the centre and sides of the gâteau with toasted flaked almonds and top each meringue rosette with a gooseberry.

Cook's Tip

In order to achieve a light sponge, when folding in the ingredients use a metal tablespoon and work quickly and lightly. An uncooked sponge mixture must be put into the preheated oven without delay.

Caribbean Coconut Cake

SPONGE MIXTURE
4 eggs, separated
2 tablespoons lukewarm water
140 g/4½ oz castor sugar
grated rind of ½ lemon
120 g/4 oz plain flour
60 g/2 oz cornflour
1 teaspoon baking powder
FILLING AND TOPPING
1 coconut or 225 g/8 oz
   desiccated coconut
2 tablespoons coconut milk
40 g/1½ oz sugar
1 tablespoon dark rum
25 g/1 oz cornflour
300 ml/½ pint milk
3 eggs, separated
180 g/6 oz castor sugar
¼ teaspoon vanilla essence
16 glacé cherries

Grease the base of a 20-cm/8-inch springform cake tin. Preheat the oven to moderately hot (190°C, 375°F, Gas Mark 5).

Whisk the egg yolks with the water, half the sugar and the lemon rind until creamy. Whisk the egg whites until stiff, fold in the remaining sugar and carefully fold into the egg yolk mixture. Sift the flour with the cornflour and baking powder and fold into the egg mixture. Turn into the prepared tin, smooth the surface and bake for 35–40 minutes. Allow to cool slightly in the tin then turn on to a wire rack to cool completely. Leave overnight if possible, then cut into three layers.

Pierce the coconut twice at the thinnest part of the shell, pour off the milk and reserve. Cut the coconut in half, scoop out the flesh, cover and reserve. Boil 2 tablespoons of the coconut milk with the 40 g/1½ oz

sugar until the sugar dissolves completely. Add the rum and leave to cool. (If using desiccated coconut, 100 g/4 oz of this should be infused in 300 ml/½ pint boiling water overnight, then strained. This liquid may be used instead of the fresh coconut milk.)

Blend the cornflour with 3 tablespoons fresh milk and the egg yolks. Heat the remaining fresh milk with half the castor sugar until almost boiling. Whisk the egg whites until stiff then carefully fold in the rest of the castor sugar. Pour the hot milk on to the cornflour mixture. Return to the heat and bring to the boil, stirring continuously. Remove from the heat, stir in the vanilla essence, cool for 5 minutes and carefully fold in the whisked egg whites.

Allow this vanilla cream to cool slightly then spread thickly over the bottom cake layer. Place the second cake layer on

top, sprinkle over half the coconut milk mixture and allow it to soak in. Spread over a layer of the cream then top with the last cake layer. Sprinkle over the rest of the coconut milk, allowing it to soak in, and then spread the top and sides of the cake with the remaining vanilla cream.

Grate the coconut flesh finely and use to cover the cake thickly all over. Alternatively, use the remaining desiccated coconut. Arrange the glacé cherries around the edge of the cake.

From the Cake Tray

Danish Scrolls

YEAST PASTRY DOUGH
450 g/1 lb plain flour
30 g/1 oz fresh yeast
250 ml/8 fl oz lukewarm milk
225 g/8 oz butter
1 egg
½ teaspoon salt
FILLING
2 tablespoons soft brown sugar
¼ teaspoon ground cinnamon
50 g/2 oz raisins

Sift the flour into a bowl and make a well. Cream the yeast with the milk and pour into the flour well. Sprinkle over a little flour, cover and leave for 15 minutes, until frothy. Melt 50 g/2 oz butter and add to the bowl with the egg and salt. Beat all to a smooth dough and knead. Cover and leave to rise for 15 minutes.

Roll out the dough to a 20 × 35-cm/8 × 14-inch oblong and mark into three sections. Dot half the remaining butter over the top two sections and fold the bottom section over the middle section. Fold the top section down over this. Press the edges firmly together, turn the dough once in an anticlockwise direction and carefully roll out to an oblong 20 × 35 cm/8 × 14 inches. Repeat this process using the remaining butter, then repeat once more without using any butter. Chill for 15 minutes between each rolling.

Preheat the oven to 200°C, 400°F, Gas Mark 6. Roll out the pastry to measure 35 × 50 cm/14 × 20 inches, and brush with water. Spread over the mixed sugar, cinnamon and raisins and from the long sides roll the pastry in to meet at the centre. Cut into 2·5-cm/ 1-inch slices and place flat on greased baking trays. Bake for 10 minutes then reduce to 180°C, 350°F, Gas Mark 4 for 10–15 minutes.

Hazelnut Combs

1 (212-g/7½-oz) packet frozen puff pastry
1 egg yolk, beaten to glaze
FILLING
150 g/5 oz ground hazelnuts
1 egg, beaten
80 g/3 oz castor sugar
1 tablespoon rum

Allow the pastry to thaw for 1 hour at room temperature.

Roll out the pastry on a floured surface to make a 30-cm/12-inch square. Cut out nine 10-cm/4-inch squares. Mix together the hazelnuts, beaten egg, sugar and rum. Place a strip of this nut filling down the centre of each square. Brush one side of each square with the beaten egg yolk and fold over the opposite side. Make even cuts along this sealed edge and spread a little to form a comb.

Sprinkle a large baking tray with cold water and place the hazelnut combs on it. Brush the tops with beaten egg yolk and leave to stand in the refrigerator for 15 minutes. Preheat the oven to hot (220°C, 425°F, Gas Mark 7). Bake the hazelnut combs for 15 minutes, then cool on a wire rack.

From the Cake Tray

Hazelnut Pastries

YEAST PASTRY DOUGH
500 g/1 lb 2 oz plain flour
30 g/1 oz fresh yeast
250 ml/8 fl oz lukewarm milk
225 g/8 oz butter
1 egg
¼ teaspoon salt
FILLING
100 g/4 oz toasted hazelnuts,
ground
50 g/2 oz castor sugar
2 tablespoons rum
¼ teaspoon almond essence
1 egg white
GLAZE
3 tablespoons icing sugar
1–2 teaspoons rum

Prepare the yeast pastry dough according to the recipe for Danish Scrolls (see page 49). Work the remaining 50 g/2 oz flour into the remaining 175 g/ 6 oz butter; chill, fold and roll with the yeast dough, as described in the same recipe.

Roll and fold three times in all, allowing to rest in the refrigerator in between each rolling.

Preheat the oven to hot (220°C, 425°F, Gas Mark 7). Finally divide the dough in half and roll out each piece to measure 23 × 55 cm/9 × 22 inches.

Mix the hazelnuts, sugar, rum, almond essence and egg white together, and spread over one of the pastry rectangles. Place the other pastry rectangle over this and press the edges firmly together to seal. Cut widthways into 2·5-cm/1-inch wide pieces, make a 7·5-cm/ 3-inch long slit near one end of each piece and carefully twist the other end before pulling it through this opening (see illustration). Seal the ends together well. Place on a baking tray and bake for 15 minutes.

Mix the sifted icing sugar with the rum and use to glaze the pastries while still warm.

Orange Almond Croissants

YEAST PASTRY DOUGH
450 g/1 lb plain flour
30 g/1 oz fresh yeast
250 ml/8 fl oz lukewarm milk
225 g/8 oz butter
1 egg
¼ teaspoon salt
FILLING
175 g/6 oz ground almonds
grated rind and juice of 1 orange
2 tablespoons orange liqueur
30 g/1 oz candied orange peel,
finely chopped
1 egg white
GLAZE
1 egg yolk, beaten
3 tablespoons icing sugar
1 tablespoon orange juice
50 g/2 oz toasted flaked almonds

Prepare and roll the yeast dough according to the recipe for Danish Scrolls (see page 49). Finally roll out the dough to a 40 × 50-cm/16 × 20-inch rectangle.

Mix the ground almonds with the rest of the filling ingredients. Cut the dough into four 10 × 50-cm/4 × 20-inch strips, then cut each strip into five to give 10-cm/4-inch squares. Cut each square in half diagonally to give triangles with two sides measuring 10 cm/4 inches each. Place a little of the filling in the centre of each triangle and roll up from the long side. Place on greased baking trays and leave to rise for 15 minutes in a warm place. Preheat the oven to hot (220°C, 425°F, Gas Mark 7).

Brush the croissants with beaten egg yolk and bake for 15–20 minutes. While still hot, glaze with the mixed icing sugar and orange juice, and sprinkle with flaked almonds.

Cream-Filled Choux Puffs

CHOUX PASTE
250 ml/8 fl oz water
60 g/2 oz butter or margarine
pinch of salt
grated rind of ½ lemon
200 g/7 oz plain flour
4 eggs, beaten
FILLING
450 ml/¾ pint double cream
60 g/2 oz castor sugar
icing sugar to sprinkle

In a heavy-based pan gently heat the water with the butter or margarine, salt and lemon rind, until the fat is melted. Bring to the boil then tip in the sifted flour all at once, remove from the heat and beat well until the ingredients form a ball and come away from the sides of the pan. Return to the heat and cook for 1 minute, stirring all the time. Turn the mixture into a bowl, allow to cool slightly then add the eggs a little at a time, beating well with each addition.

Preheat the oven to hot (220°C, 425°F, Gas Mark 7). Pipe the choux paste in different shapes on to a baking tray, leaving sufficient space between each to allow for rising during cooking. Bake for 20 minutes. Do not open the oven door during the first 10 minutes' baking time, or the pastry will collapse.

While the choux puffs are still warm, split through to let any steam escape. Allow to cool. Whip the cream stiffly with the sugar and pipe into each puff. Dust the tops with icing sugar.

Cook's Tip

You can pipe long éclair shapes from the choux paste, then fill these with coffee cream and ice with a coffee icing.

Chocolate Slice

CAKE MIXTURE
130 g/5 oz plain chocolate
130 g/5 oz butter
200 g/7 oz castor sugar
pinch each of salt, ground
   cinnamon and grated lemon
   rind
6 eggs, separated
130 g/5 oz plain flour
ICING
200 g/7 oz plain chocolate
2 eggs
400 g/14 oz icing sugar
120 g/4 oz coconut oil or butter
3 tablespoons rum

Line a 25 × 35-cm/10 × 14-inch Swiss roll tin with greased greaseproof paper. Preheat the oven to moderate (180°C, 350°F, Gas Mark 4).

Melt the chocolate in a basin over hot water. Cream the butter with half the sugar until light and fluffy. Add the salt, cinnamon and lemon rind, then beat in the egg yolks, one at a time, with the melted chocolate. Whisk the egg whites until stiff and fold in the remaining sugar. Fold into the creamed mixture with the sifted flour. Spread evenly into the Swiss roll tin and bake in the centre of the oven for 20 minutes.

Turn the cake out on to greaseproof paper sprinkled with sugar, remove the greaseproof lining paper and leave to cool for 2 hours. Cut the cake lengthways into two strips.

Grate the chocolate finely and mix with the beaten eggs, sifted icing sugar, melted coconut oil or butter, and rum. Heat gently in a basin over a pan of boiling water, stirring until the chocolate melts and all the ingredients are thoroughly combined. Cool. Use to sandwich the strips of cake together and spread thickly over the top. Cut into slices when the icing is firm.

Nougat Slice

SPONGE MIXTURE
4 eggs, separated, plus 2 egg
   yolks
100 g/4 oz castor sugar
80 g/3 oz plain flour
20 g/1 oz cornflour
40 g/1½ oz cocoa powder
FILLING AND ICING
25 g/1 oz cornflour
2 egg yolks
50 g/2 oz castor sugar
300 ml/½ pint milk
250 g/9 oz butter
100 g/4 oz nougat
175 g/6 oz plain chocolate
glacé cherries to decorate

Line a 33 × 23-cm/13 × 9-inch Swiss roll tin with greased greaseproof. Preheat the oven to 220°C, 425°F, Gas Mark 7.

Whisk the egg yolks with half the sugar until pale. Whisk the egg whites until stiff and fold in the remaining sugar. Fold into the egg yolks. Sift the flour, cornflour and cocoa powder and fold in. Spread over the Swiss roll tin and bake for 10–12 minutes. Turn out on to clean greaseproof and peel off the lining paper. Cool then cut lengthways into three strips.

Blend the cornflour with the egg yolks, sugar and a little milk. Heat the remaining milk, stir into the cornflour mixture and return to the heat. Bring to the boil, stirring until thickened. Leave to cool. Cream the butter until pale and soft, then gradually beat in the cornflour sauce. Melt the nougat with 50 g/2 oz of the chocolate in a basin over hot water, then beat into the butter cream a tablespoon at a time. Spread this nougat cream over two of the strips of cake, then place the strips on top of each other and spread a thin layer of nougat cream over the top and sides.

Melt the remaining chocolate and ice the cake. Decorate as illustrated.

Shortbread Fingers

320 g/11 oz butter
180 g/6 oz castor sugar
¼ teaspoon salt
500 g/1 lb 2 oz plain flour
castor sugar to sprinkle

Cream the butter with the sugar and salt until pale and fluffy. Sift the flour and knead into the creamed ingredients to give a workable dough. Cover and leave for 2 hours in the refrigerator.

Preheat the oven to moderately hot (190°C, 375°F, Gas Mark 5). Roll out the mixture on a floured surface until 1·5 cm/¾ inch thick and place on a greased baking tray. Prick several times with a fork and bake for 25–30 minutes.

Whilst still warm, cut the shortbread into fingers with a sharp knife and sprinkle with castor sugar.

Teacakes

Prepare these using the recipe for Bath Buns (see left), but use 1 teaspoon of sugar to sweeten the mixture instead of 80 g/ 3 oz. Leave out the aniseed, cinnamon and lemon rind. Instead of using mixed peel and raisins, add 150 g/5 oz currants. Brush the risen teacakes with egg yolk before baking.

Finger Biscuits

4 eggs, separated, plus 2 egg
  yolks
125 g/4½ oz castor sugar
50 g/2 oz cornflour
100 g/4 oz plain flour
icing sugar to sprinkle

Grease non-stick baking trays
or line ordinary baking trays
with non-stick baking parchment and grease well. Preheat
the oven to moderately hot
(200°C, 400°F, Gas Mark 6).

Whisk all the egg yolks with
the sugar until pale and creamy.
Whisk the egg whites until stiff
and carefully fold into the egg
yolk mixture. Finally fold in
the sifted cornflour and flour.

Fill a piping bag fitted with a
large plain nozzle with this
biscuit dough. Pipe 8·5-cm/
3½-inch long fingers on to the
baking trays, allowing space
between each one for the mixture to spread during cooking.

Bake the biscuits for 7–10
minutes, until light golden
brown.

Allow to cool for a few
seconds on the baking trays
then transfer to a wire rack.
Sprinkle with sifted icing sugar
when cooled.

Cook's Tip

Using the same mixture,
you can pipe round
biscuits. When cool join
two together with melted
chocolate and decorate
the top of each pair with
a blob of chocolate.

Almond Macaroons

225 g/8 oz ground almonds
225 g/8 oz castor sugar
4 egg whites

Line one or two baking trays
with rice paper. Preheat the
oven to moderate (160°C,
325°F, Gas Mark 3).

Mix the ground almonds
with the sugar and unbeaten
egg whites, stirring to a smooth
mixture. Fill a piping bag fitted
with a plain nozzle with the
mixture and pipe small rounds
on to the rice paper, leaving
enough room for them to
spread during cooking. Bake
the macaroons for 15–20
minutes.

Leave to cool on the rice
paper, then cut round to trim
off excess paper.

Cook's Tip

These macaroons can
also be made with
ground hazelnuts instead
of almonds; for the best
possible taste use lightly
roasted nuts.

Marzipan Toasts

500 g/1 lb plain flour
30 g/1 oz fresh yeast
250 ml/8 fl oz lukewarm milk
50 g/2 oz butter or margarine
50 g/2 oz castor sugar
¼ teaspoon salt
grated rind of ½ lemon
2 eggs
TOPPING
100 g/4 oz ground almonds
80 g/3 oz icing sugar
1 egg white
1 tablespoon rum

Grease two cylindrical-shaped or Balmoral cake tins, or two 0·5 kg/1-lb loaf tins.

Sift the flour into a bowl and make a well in the centre. Cream the yeast with a little of the milk. Add the remaining milk and pour into the flour. Mix in a little flour, cover and leave in a warm place for 15 minutes, until frothy.

Melt the butter or margarine and mix with the sugar, salt, lemon rind and beaten eggs. Add these to the yeast mixture and work all the ingredients to a dry dough. Knead the dough until smooth and elastic then cover and leave to rise for 15 minutes. Knead again lightly and form into two rolls on a floured surface. Shape these to fit the prepared tins and leave to rise until the loaves have doubled in size.

Preheat the oven to hot (220°C, 425°F, Gas Mark 7) and bake the loaves for 25–35 minutes, until golden brown.

Turn out to cool on a wire rack and leave overnight.

Preheat the grill to the hottest setting. Cut the cooled loaves into thick slices, arrange them on the grill pan and toast on one side. Leave to cool. Meanwhile mix the ground almonds with the sifted icing sugar, egg white and rum, to make a smooth spreading consistency. Spread this mixture on to the untoasted sides of the bread slices and toast until lightly browned.

Cook's Tip

If you are in a hurry, use bought almond paste kneaded with a little rum.

These Marzipan Toasts make a delicious and speedy snack to serve at teatime or with morning coffee.

Turkish Fruit Cake

175 g/6 oz butter
100 g/4 oz castor sugar
1 tablespoon vanilla sugar
grated rind of 1 lemon
4 eggs
1 tablespoon Madeira
175 g/6 oz self-raising flour
50 g/2 oz cornflour
1 teaspoon baking powder
75 g/3 oz raisins
75 g/3 oz glacé cherries, washed
*   and roughly chopped*
100 g/4 oz pickled walnuts,
*   roughly chopped*
¼ teaspoon salt
½ teaspoon ground cinnamon
½ teaspoon ground cardamom
ICING
100 g/4 oz plain chocolate
50 g/2 oz pistachio nuts, chopped

Grease a 1-kg/2-lb loaf tin and
sprinkle with fine breadcrumbs.
Preheat the oven to moderate
(180°C, 350°F, Gas Mark 4).

Cream the butter, sugar,
vanilla sugar and lemon rind
together until pale and soft.
Stir in the eggs and Madeira.
Sift the flour, cornflour and
baking powder together and
mix in the raisins, cherries,
pickled walnuts, salt, cinnamon
and cardamom. Fold this flour
mixture into the creamed mixture and turn into the prepared
tin. Bake for about 1 hour 5
minutes then turn on to a wire
rack to cool.

Melt the chocolate in a basin
over a pan of hot water and use
to ice the cake all over.
Decorate with the chopped
pistachios before the icing sets.

Rum Butter Cake

180 g/6 oz butter
200 g/7 oz castor sugar
5 eggs
250 g/9 oz plain flour
80 g/3 oz maize flour
1 teaspoon baking powder
3 tablespoons rum
1 tablespoon lemon juice
1 tablespoon orange juice
grated rind of ½ lemon
grated rind of ½ orange

Grease a 1-kg/2-lb loaf tin and sprinkle with flour. Preheat the oven to moderately hot (190°C, 375°F, Gas Mark 5).

Beat the butter and sugar until pale and creamy then add the eggs one at a time. Sift the flour, maize flour and baking powder together then carefully fold into the mixture. Gradually fold in the rum, lemon and orange juice and grated fruit rinds. Place the mixture in the tin, smooth over the top and bake for 1¼ hours. Cover with foil if becoming too brown.

Turn out on to a wire rack to cool.

Royal Fruit Loaf

50 g/2 oz candied lemon peel
100 g/4 oz blanched almonds
200 g/7 oz raisins
175 g/6 oz self-raising flour
175 g/6 oz butter or margarine
100 g/4 oz castor sugar
4 eggs
50 g/2 oz cornflour
1 teaspoon baking powder
1 tablespoon rum

Grease a 0·5-kg/1-lb loaf tin and sprinkle with fine bread-crumbs. Preheat the oven to moderate (180°C, 350°F, Gas Mark 4).

Chop the lemon peel and almonds. Toss the raisins in a little of the flour. Beat the butter or margarine with the sugar until pale and creamy, then beat in one of the eggs. Sift the flour, cornflour and baking powder together and fold in a little of this between adding the remaining eggs. Fold in the rest of the flour. Add the lemon peel, almonds, raisins and rum and fold into the creamed mixture. Place in the prepared tin, smooth over the surface and bake for about 1 hour 5 minutes.

Turn the cake on to a wire rack to cool.

Teatime Treats

Crumble Puffs

1 (368-g/13-oz) packet frozen
   puff pastry
1 egg yolk
TOPPING
200 g/7 oz plain flour
100 g/3½ oz castor sugar
pinch of ground cinnamon
pinch of salt
150 g/5 oz butter
icing sugar to sprinkle

Allow the pastry to thaw for
1 hour at room temperature.
   Roll out the pastry on a
floured surface and cut into
5-cm/2-inch rounds. Then roll
in one direction only until
about 11·5 cm/4½ inches long
and leaf-shaped. Sprinkle a
baking tray with cold water,
arrange the elongated leaves on
it and brush with beaten egg
yolk. Leave to rest for 15
minutes. Preheat the oven to
moderately hot (200°C, 400°F,
Gas Mark 6).

Mix the sifted flour with the
sugar, cinnamon and salt. Melt
the butter and add to the dry
ingredients drop by drop, stirring continuously with the
blade of a knife. Rub the mixture to a crumble consistency
with the hands. Sprinkle this
over the leaves and bake for
12–15 minutes, until crisp and
brown.
   Leave the cooled crumble
puffs on a wire rack to become
completely cold then sprinkle
with sifted icing sugar.

Chinese Doughnuts

25 g/1 oz butter or margarine
175 g/6 oz castor sugar
1 egg
2 tablespoons water
350 g/12 oz plain flour
1 teaspoon baking powder
75 g/3 oz sesame seeds
oil or fat to deep fry

Mix the butter or margarine
with the sugar, then beat in the
egg and water until light. Sift
the flour with the baking
powder and work into the
mixture. Knead the dough well
and form into a 50-cm/20-inch
long roll. Cut 2·5-cm/1-inch
slices from the roll. Shape these
into small balls, dip them
briefly into cold water then toss
them in the sesame seeds.
   Heat the cooking oil or fat to
182°C/360°F. Cook 6–8
doughnuts at a time, turning
frequently, for about 5 minutes
until golden brown. Remove
from the hot fat with a draining
spoon and drain on absorbent
paper.

Butter Swirls

375 g/13 oz plain flour
250 g/9 oz butter, cut into flakes
125 g/4½ oz castor sugar
6 egg yolks
pinch of salt
grated rind of ¼ lemon
sugar crystals to sprinkle

Sift the flour into a bowl and dot with the butter. Form a well in the centre of the flour and add the sugar, 5 egg yolks, the salt and lemon rind. Knead all the ingredients together to obtain a smooth dough. Place the mixture in a piping bag fitted with a plain nozzle and at equal intervals pipe 'S' shapes on to two greased baking trays. Leave for 1 hour in a cool place.

Preheat the oven to moderately hot (190°C, 375°F, Gas Mark 5). Beat the remaining egg yolk and use to brush the biscuits. While still moist sprinkle with sugar crystals. If any sugar falls on to the baking tray remove with a pastry brush to avoid burning. Bake the biscuits for 8–10 minutes until golden.

Allow the biscuits to cool on the baking trays for about 5 minutes, then remove with a palette knife and leave until completely cool on a wire rack.

Aniseed Chräbeli

250 g/9 oz plain flour
250 g/9 oz castor sugar
2 eggs
1–2 teaspoons ground aniseed
grated rind of ¼ lemon

Sift the flour into a bowl. Beat the sugar with the eggs until creamy and mix in the flour with a spoon. Finally add the aniseed and lemon rind. Form the dough into rolls of finger thickness. Cut the rolls into 7·5-cm/3-inch lengths and form each piece into a half-moon shape. Slit the outer edges of the half-moons three times horizontally with a sharp knife. Place on a floured baking tray, cover and leave to stand overnight at room temperature.

Preheat the oven to moderately hot (190°C, 375°F, Gas Mark 5) and bake for 12–15 minutes on the middle shelf. Remove from the baking tray while still warm and cool on a wire rack.

Cook's Tip

Half-moons are the traditional shape for Chräbeli. To save time you can simply cut the rolls into equal thick slices, make slits in these and continue as in the recipe.

Teatime Treats

Chocolate Almond Bars

250 g/9 oz butter
150 g/5 oz icing sugar
2 eggs
2 tablespoons milk
grated rind of 1 lemon
520 g/1 lb 2 oz plain flour
200 g/7 oz blanched almonds,
    coarsely chopped
TOPPING
100 g/4 oz plain chocolate
200 g/7 oz blanched almonds,
    cut into strips

Beat the butter, sifted icing sugar, eggs, milk and lemon rind together. Sift the flour and knead well into the butter mixture with the chopped almonds, to give a workable dough. Roll out half the dough with your hands, to make a long thin roll, about 2·5 cm/1 inch in width, and then press flat, to give a strip of dough about 3·5 cm/ 1½ inches wide. Wrap in foil or cling film and leave for 2 hours in the refrigerator. Similarly roll and chill the remaining portion of dough.

Preheat the oven to moderately hot (200°C, 400°F, Gas Mark 6). Cut the strips of dough into pieces 6 cm/2½ inches long. Place these biscuits on greased baking trays and bake for 15 minutes, until golden brown. Allow to cool slightly before transferring to a wire rack with a palette knife.

Melt the chocolate in a basin over hot water and spread thickly over the biscuits. While the chocolate is still soft, toast the almond strips and sprinkle over. Allow the chocolate to set before storing the biscuits in an airtight container.

Sugar Pretzels

20 g/¾ oz fresh yeast
125 ml/4 fl oz lukewarm milk
80 g/3 oz butter or margarine
1 egg
½ teaspoon salt
pinch of ground cardamom
320 g/11 oz plain flour
1 egg yolk, beaten to glaze
50 g/2 oz sugar crystals to
    decorate

Lightly grease a baking tray with butter or margarine.

Cream the yeast with the milk. Melt the butter and stir in the beaten egg, salt and cardamom. Sift the flour into a bowl, make a well in the centre and pour in the yeast and the butter mixture. Mix all together to a firm dough. Knead until smooth but do not leave to rise. Preheat the oven to hot (230°C, 450°F, Gas Mark 8).

Roll out the dough on a lightly floured surface to make a thick long roll. Cut into 24 equal pieces and roll out each piece into a long thin strip, approximately 40 cm/16 inches in length. Form the strips into pretzel shapes, as illustrated. Brush these with beaten egg yolk and press the sugar crystals on to one side to decorate. Place on the tray and bake for 8–10 minutes.

Remove from the baking tray carefully and allow to cool on a wire rack. These pretzels taste best served fresh.

Orange and Nutmeg Biscuits

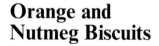

150 g/5 oz butter
100 g/4 oz castor sugar
pinch of salt
generous pinch of grated nutmeg
grated rind of 1 orange
2 egg yolks
250 g/9 oz plain flour
75 g/3 oz sugar crystals

Beat together the butter, sugar, salt, nutmeg, orange rind and 1 egg yolk, until pale and creamy. Add the sifted flour and knead in thoroughly to give a workable dough. Form the mixture into a roll measuring 4 cm/1¾ inches in diameter. Cover with foil and leave in the refrigerator for 2 hours.

Preheat the oven to moderately hot (200°C, 400°F, Gas Mark 6).

Beat the second egg yolk.

Brush the roll of dough with this and coat it all over with the sugar crystals, pressing in well. Cut into slices about 5 mm/¼ inch thick and lay flat on greased baking trays, leaving a little space between each one. Bake the biscuits for 12–15 minutes, until light brown.

Allow the biscuits to cool for 5 minutes, then carefully remove from the baking trays with a palette knife and cool completely on a wire rack.

Cats' Tongues

250 g/9 oz butter
220 g/8 oz icing sugar
¼ teaspoon vanilla essence
pinch of salt
1 egg plus 1 egg yolk
250 g/9 oz plain flour
ICING
100 g/4 oz nougat
75 g/3 oz plain chocolate

Grease two baking trays and dust with flour. Preheat the oven to moderately hot (200°C, 400°F, Gas Mark 6).

Beat the butter, sifted icing sugar, vanilla essence and salt together until pale and creamy. Beat in the egg and egg yolk separately and finally fold in the sifted flour. Using a piping bag fitted with a plain nozzle, pipe the biscuit mixture on to the trays. Shape into cats' tongues as you pipe (see illustration) and make each one about 7·5 cm/3 inches in

length. Leave enough space between each to allow for spreading during baking. Bake for 8–12 minutes, until golden brown, then transfer to a wire rack and allow to cool.

Melt the nougat with the chocolate in a basin over hot water. Spread this icing over the cats' tongues, pressing pairs lightly together (see illustration). Allow the nougat icing to harden before storing in an airtight tin.

Austrian Marble Cake

250 g/9 oz soft margarine
200 g/7 oz castor sugar
4 eggs
6 tablespoons milk
400 g/14 oz plain flour
100 g/4 oz cornflour
2 teaspoons baking powder
40 g/1½ oz cocoa powder
40 g/1¼ oz icing sugar
icing sugar to sprinkle

Grease two small fluted savarin tins, each measuring 18 cm/ 7 inches in diameter, and sprinkle with fine breadcrumbs. Preheat the oven to moderately hot (200°C, 400°F, Gas Mark 6).

Beat the margarine and castor sugar together until pale and creamy. Beat in the eggs one by one, and finally add the milk. Sift the flour with the cornflour and baking powder and carefully fold into the creamed mixture.

Divide the mixture into two equal portions and half-fill the prepared tins with one portion. Mix the remaining portion with the sifted cocoa powder and icing sugar, and divide this also between both tins. Lightly blend the two mixtures in the tins by swirling carefully with a skewer. Place in the oven and bake for 1–1¼ hours.

Allow to cool on a wire rack then dust with sifted icing sugar.

Candied Fruit Loaf

300 g/11 oz plain flour
pinch of salt
30 g/1 oz fresh yeast
6 tablespoons lukewarm milk
400 g/14 oz candied fruit
(cherries, angelica, pineapple, ginger, finely chopped)
80 g/3 oz soft margarine
50 g/2 oz castor sugar
4 eggs

Grease two 0·5-kg/1-lb loaf tins and sprinkle with flour.

Sift the flour and salt into a bowl. Cream the yeast with a little of the milk then add the remaining milk. Stir the candied fruit into the flour then make a well in the centre and pour in the yeast liquid. Sprinkle over a little flour and leave in a warm place for 15 minutes, until frothy.

Beat the margarine with the sugar and eggs and add to the bowl. Beat all the ingredients well together until bubbles appear. Cover and leave to rise in a warm place for a further 30 minutes. Beat well again and divide between the two tins. Stand in a warm place until the mixture has risen to approximately 1 cm/½ inch below the top of the tin. Preheat the oven to moderately hot (200°C, 400°F, Gas Mark 6).

Bake for 30–35 minutes then turn out to cool on a wire rack.

Fruit Flans

PASTRY
60 g/2 oz soft margarine
45 g/1½ oz icing sugar
few drops of vanilla essence
pinch of salt
1 small egg yolk
125 g/4½ oz plain flour
TOPPING
50 g/2 oz ground almonds
1 tablespoon rum
2 tablespoons sugar syrup
675 g/1½ lb prepared fresh or
drained canned fruit
1 small packet quick-setting jel
mix (lemon)
50 g/2 oz toasted flaked almonds

Knead together the margarine, sifted icing sugar, vanilla essence, salt, egg yolk and sifted flour. Wrap in foil or cling film and leave for 2 hours in the refrigerator.

Preheat the oven to moderately hot (200°C, 400°F, Gas Mark 6). Roll out the pastry on a floured surface to line the base of two 15-cm/6-inch flan tins. Bake blind for 15 minutes then allow to cool on a wire rack.

Mix the ground almonds with the rum and syrup, and spread over the pastry bases and sides. Arrange the prepared fruit attractively on top. Prepare the quick-setting jel mix, following the instructions on the packet, and pour over the fruit. Finally decorate the sides of the flans with toasted flaked almonds, pressing them in well.

Iced Lemon Cake

CAKE MIXTURE
125 g/4½ oz soft margarine
grated rind of 1 lemon
100 g/4 oz castor sugar
2 eggs
3 tablespoons milk
200 g/7 oz self-raising flour
50 g/2 oz cornflour
¼ teaspoon baking powder
SYRUP
2 tablespoons water
juice of 1 lemon
50 g/2 oz sugar
1 tablespoon arrack or ouzo
ICING
100 g/4 oz icing sugar
2 tablespoons lemon juice
strip of lemon peel

Grease a 20-cm/8-inch round cake tin and sprinkle with fine breadcrumbs. Preheat the oven to moderately hot (190°C, 375°F, Gas Mark 5).

Beat together the margarine, lemon rind and sugar until pale and creamy. Stir in the eggs and milk then fold in the sifted flour, cornflour and baking powder. Turn into the prepared cake tin, smooth over the surface, and bake for 40–50 minutes. Turn on to a wire rack to cool.

Bring the water to the boil with the lemon juice and sugar. Add the arrack or ouzo and pour slowly over the cake, allowing the syrup to soak well in.

Mix the sifted icing sugar with the lemon juice until smooth and spread thickly on top of the cake, allowing it to fall over the sides. Shred the strip of lemon peel and sprinkle over the icing before it sets.

Quiche Lorraine

PASTRY
200 g/7 oz plain flour
¼ teaspoon salt
100 g/3½ oz butter or margarine,
  cut into flakes
2–3 tablespoons water
FILLING
225 g/8 oz streaky bacon
4 eggs, separated
250 ml/8 fl oz single cream
pinch of white pepper
¼ teaspoon salt
125 g/4½ oz Edam cheese, grated

Grease and flour one loose-bottomed 25-cm/10-inch flan tin or two 18-cm/7-inch tins.

Sift the flour and salt into a mixing bowl and add the butter and water. Knead to a dough. Wrap the pastry in foil or cling film and leave in the refrigerator for 2 hours.

Preheat the oven to moderately hot (200°C, 400°F, Gas Mark 6). Roll out the pastry on a floured surface to about 4 mm/⅙ inch thick and use to line the base and sides of the flan tin. Prick the base of the pastry all over with a fork.

Coarsely chop the bacon rashers and scatter over the pastry base. Whisk the egg yolks with the cream, pepper and salt, and mix in the grated cheese. Whisk the egg whites until stiff and fold into the cheese mixture. Pour into the pastry case, smooth the surface and bake for 30–40 minutes.

When cooked, allow the quiche to cool for a while in the tin, then transfer to a serving plate and cut while still warm. Accompany the quiche with wine – a dry white Alsace is especially good.

Cook's Tip

Bacon, combined with eggs and cream, is the traditional filling for a Quiche Lorraine. Equally delicious quiche fillings include smoked or flaked fresh salmon, mushrooms tossed in a little butter, cooked chopped spinach or drained canned asparagus spears.

To Serve with Drinks

Crispy Cheese Biscuits

150 g/5 oz butter
180 g/6 oz Gruyère or
Emmenthal cheese, grated
6 tablespoons single cream
¼ teaspoon salt
1 teaspoon paprika pepper
½ teaspoon baking powder
250 g/9 oz plain flour
1 egg yolk, beaten to glaze
TOPPING
poppy seeds, sesame seeds,
caraway seeds, chopped
pistachio nuts, blanched
almonds

Soften the butter with a wooden spoon. Gradually add the cheese and beat thoroughly. Stir in the cream, salt and paprika. Sift the baking powder with the flour and stir into the mixture. Knead lightly to incorporate all the flour and give a smooth dough. Cut the dough into two or three pieces, wrap in kitchen foil or cling film and leave for 2 hours in the refrigerator.

Preheat the oven to moderately hot (200°C, 400°F, Gas Mark 6). On a floured board roll out the pieces of dough one at a time to a thickness of about 5 mm/¼ inch. Cut into biscuits of any shape, for example rings, hearts, half-moons or stars, and place on greased baking trays. Brush with the beaten egg yolk and while still moist sprinkle with poppy seeds, sesame seeds, caraway seeds or chopped pistachios, or top with a halved almond. Bake the biscuits for 10–15 minutes.

While the cheese biscuits are still hot remove carefully from the baking trays with a palette knife and leave until warm on a wire rack. Serve warm.

Cook's Tip

There is also an Italian variety of these biscuits made with Gorgonzola cheese. Make the biscuits as in the given recipe and sprinkle half with sesame seeds. Bake as above. Finely grate 75 g/3 oz Gorgonzola cheese and mix with 125 g/5 oz cream cheese, 1 egg yolk, a pinch of salt and cayenne pepper, and 1 teaspoon paprika pepper. Fill a piping bag with the cream cheese mixture and with a star nozzle decorate the remaining cooked biscuits.

Surprise Sausage Flan

1 (368-g/13-oz) packet frozen
   puff pastry
FILLING
1 onion, sliced
2 tablespoons oil
1 clove garlic, crushed
½ teaspoon salt
¼ teaspoon black pepper
100 g/4 oz minced beef
100 g/4 oz minced pork
2 tablespoons fresh white
   breadcrumbs
few drops of anchovy essence
2 beef or pork sausages
50 g/2 oz garlic sausage, sliced
2 eggs
1 teaspoon dried marjoram
¼ teaspoon dried thyme
3 tablespoons milk

Allow the pastry to thaw for
1 hour at room temperature.
Roll out on a floured surface
and use to line a 23-cm/9-inch

flan ring or tin. Preheat the
oven to moderately hot (200°C,
400°F, Gas Mark 6).
   Fry the onion in the oil until
soft. Add the garlic, salt and
pepper and fry for a further 5
minutes. Mix together the
minced beef and pork, the
breadcrumbs, anchovy essence
and the onion mixture. Spread
into the pastry case. Grill or
fry the sausages until well
browned, then slice. Arrange
the sausage and garlic sausage
slices over the minced meat
mixture. Whisk the eggs with
the herbs and milk and pour
over. Bake for 40 minutes and
serve hot.

Savoury Upside-Down Pie

1 (212-g/7½-oz) packet frozen
   puff pastry
TOPPING
675 g/1½ lb minced beef
1 teaspoon salt
¼ teaspoon black pepper
1 large onion, chopped
3 egg yolks
100 g/4 oz mushrooms
50 g/2 oz blue cheese
100 g/4 oz streaky bacon rashers
1½ tablespoons each chopped
   sorrel and chervil

Allow the pastry to thaw for
1 hour at room temperature.
   Mix the minced beef with the
salt, pepper and onion; bind
with the egg yolks. Wash and
quarter the mushrooms and
crumble the cheese. Preheat the
oven to moderately hot (200°C,
400°F, Gas Mark 6).
   Cover the base of a 20-cm/

8-inch loose-bottomed cake tin
with the streaky bacon.
Arrange the cheese, herbs and
mushrooms on top. Cover with
the meat mixture, pressing it
down firmly and smoothing the
top.
   Roll out the pastry on a
floured surface to a circle large
enough to cover the filling.
Place over the filling and prick
the pastry with a fork. Bake for
40–50 minutes. Remove from
the oven, invert the tin over a
warm plate or wire rack and
turn out the pie.

To Serve with Drinks

Spicy Meat Pie

PASTRY
350 g/12 oz plain flour
150 g/5 oz butter or margarine,
   cut into flakes
1 egg yolk
6 tablespoons lukewarm water
1 teaspoon salt
1 egg, beaten to glaze
FILLING
1 bread roll
6 tablespoons hot milk
1 onion
50 g/2 oz streaky bacon
350 g/12 oz minced pork and veal
1 tablespoon chopped parsley
6 tablespoons single cream
pinch each of salt, white pepper,
   cayenne pepper, ground
   allspice, ground cardamom
   and dried basil
¼ teaspoon grated lemon rind

Sift the flour into a mixing bowl and dot with the butter. Form a well in the centre and add the egg yolk, water and salt. Starting at the centre, knead all the ingredients quickly together to form a pastry dough. Wrap in foil or cling film and leave for 2 hours in the refrigerator.

Crumble the bread roll into a basin and spoon the milk over it. Finely chop the onion. Dice the bacon and fry with the onion until golden brown, turning continuously. In a bowl mix the minced meats with the squeezed breadcrumbs, the bacon and onion mixture, parsley, cream, seasoning, spices and lemon rind. The mixture should be highly spiced.

Preheat the oven to hot (220°C, 425°F, Gas Mark 7). Roll out two-thirds of the dough on a floured board to line a 20-cm/8-inch sandwich cake tin, leaving a border of about 3 mm/⅛ inch above the tin. Prick the pastry base in several places and spread the filling smoothly over it. Roll out the rest of the dough to the size of the tin, place over the filling and seal the edges well. Make a small hole in the centre. Brush the surface with beaten egg and pierce in several places with a skewer. From the remains of the pastry cut out flowers, leaves and stalks, and use to decorate the pie. Brush with beaten egg and bake the pie for about 1 hour. Cover with foil after 45 minutes. Place on a serving dish and serve hot.

Cook's Tip

Try the following variation occasionally. Use only 175 g/6 oz minced veal. Replace the minced pork with 175 g/6 oz finely diced calf's liver, fried lightly with a chopped onion. Add to the filling and continue as above.

Ham and Cheese Horns

1 (368-g/13-oz) packet frozen
    puff pastry
1 egg, beaten to glaze
FILLING
75 g/3 oz Gouda cheese
100 g/4 oz ham
1 egg yolk
1 tablespoon finely chopped
    parsley
1 tablespoon finely chopped
    onion
pinch each of pepper and dried
    oregano

Allow the pastry to thaw at room temperature for 1 hour.

On a floured board roll out the pastry into a sheet 58 × 25 cm/23 × 10 inches. Cut into 15 triangles, each with two very long sides (see illustration).

Finely dice the cheese and ham and mix with the egg yolk, parsley, onion, pepper and oregano. Place about 2 teaspoons of the filling towards the bottom of each triangle. Make a small cut in the short side of the triangle (see illustration) and roll the triangles into horn shapes; they should be loosely wrapped.

Sprinkle two baking trays with cold water and place the horns on them. Brush with beaten egg and leave in the refrigerator for 15 minutes. Preheat the oven to moderately hot (200°C, 400°F, Gas Mark 6) and bake the horns towards the top of the oven for 25 minutes. Serve warm.

Cook's Tip

Instead of horn shapes, the pastry may be cut into oblong pieces and used to make small rolls, which can be filled with well-seasoned minced beef instead of cheese and ham.

Cheese and Grape Puffs

2 (212-g/7½-oz) packets frozen
   puff pastry
2 eggs
2 tablespoons water
1 teaspoon paprika pepper
¼ teaspoon black pepper
1 teaspoon ground mixed spice
FILLING
225 g/8 oz Red Windsor or
   Cheddar cheese
100 g/4 oz white grapes
100 g/4 oz continental sausage,
   sliced

Allow the pastry to thaw for
1 hour at room temperature.
Preheat the oven to moderately
hot (200°C, 400°F, Gas Mark
6).

Roll out the pastry on a
floured surface to a rectangle
about 3 mm/⅛ inch thick and
cut into about forty 5-cm/2-
inch squares. Beat the eggs with
the water, paprika, black
pepper and spice, and brush
some of this mixture over the
pastry squares.

Cut the cheese into small
cubes. Halve the grapes and
remove the pips. Cut the
sausage slices into small pieces.
Place a cube of cheese, a grape
and a piece of sausage on each
pastry square. Bring the corners
of the pastry inwards to form
an envelope, and press together
firmly. Cut small rounds from
the pastry trimmings and press
on the envelopes to seal. Brush
with the remaining egg mixture.

Place on a baking tray
sprinkled with cold water and
bake in the oven for 15 minutes,
or until lightly browned. Serve
warm.

Surprise Tartlets

1 (368-g/13-oz) packet frozen
   puff pastry
FILLING
125 g/4 oz minced steak
½ teaspoon salt
½ teaspoon white pepper
1 egg
50 g/2 oz button mushrooms,
   finely chopped
50 g/2 oz Cheddar cheese, grated
50 g/2 oz liver sausage
50 g/2 oz German sausage, diced
3 tablespoons chopped parsley
75 g/3 oz walnuts, finely chopped

Allow the pastry to thaw for
1 hour at room temperature.
Sprinkle 12 small boat-
shaped and 18 round patty tins
with cold water. Preheat the
oven to moderately hot (200°C,
400°F, Gas Mark 6). Roll the
pastry out thinly and cut out to
line the patty tins. Prick the
pastry cases with a fork.

Mix the steak thoroughly
with a little salt and pepper and
the egg. Mix the mushrooms
with the cheese and liver
sausage and season lightly. Mix
the German sausage with the
parsley and walnuts and season
lightly. Use these mixtures to
fill the patty cases.

Bake the tartlets for 20
minutes and serve hot. Garnish
with tiny parsley sprigs, if
wished.

Chicken Pasties

PASTRY
250 g/9 oz plain flour
125 g/4½ oz butter
1 small egg
pinch of salt
2–3 tablespoons water
1 egg yolk, beaten to glaze
FILLING
2 soft bread rolls
about 250 ml/8 fl oz milk
50 g/2 oz ground almonds
1 egg plus 1 egg yolk
50 g/2 oz minced chicken
pinch each of salt, white pepper,
nutmeg and cayenne pepper

Knead the sifted flour with the
butter, egg, salt and water.
Cover the pastry and leave for
2 hours in the refrigerator.
  Crumble and soften the
bread in the milk. Mix the
almonds with the egg, egg yolk,
minced chicken, seasoning and
spices. Squeeze the bread rolls
and add to the mixture with

enough of the milk to give a
soft but not runny consistency.
Preheat the oven to hot (220°C,
425°F, Gas Mark 7).
  Roll out the pastry to a
thickness of 3 mm/⅛ inch. Cut
out six to eight circles measuring 10 cm/4 inches in diameter
and six to eight circles measuring 6 cm/2½ inches in diameter.
Make a hole the size of a
thimble in the centre of the
smaller circles. Line patty tins
with the larger circles and
divide the chicken mixture
between them. Brush the edges
of the smaller circles with
beaten egg yolk and place over
the filling, sealing well to the
edges. Brush the tops with egg
yolk and decorate with the leftover pastry. Bake for 20–30
minutes and serve hot.

Emmenthal Tartlets

PASTRY
250 g/9 oz plain flour
125 g/4½ oz butter, cut into
flakes
1 small egg
pinch of salt
2–3 tablespoons water
FILLING
350 g/12 oz Emmenthal cheese,
finely grated
175 ml/6 fl oz milk or cream
2 eggs
generous pinch each of white
pepper and grated nutmeg

Sift the flour into a mixing
bowl. Add the butter, egg, salt
and water, and knead to a soft
pastry dough. Wrap in foil or
cling film and leave for 2 hours
in the refrigerator.
  Preheat the oven to moderately hot (200°C, 400°F, Gas
Mark 6). Stir the cheese into

the milk or cream with the
beaten eggs and spices. Roll
out the dough on a floured
surface to a thickness of about
3 mm/⅛ inch. Cut out 16 circles,
10 cm/4 inches in diameter, and
use to line 16 patty tins. Press
down the edges well. Fill the
pastry cases to the brim with
the cheese mixture and smooth
the surface. Bake for 25–30
minutes in the centre of the
oven. These tartlets taste most
delicious served hot.

Cook's Tip

For an alternative filling,
use a mixture of 175 g/
6 oz grated cheese and
175 g/6 oz very finely
chopped ham.

Ham Pasties

*1 (368-g/13-oz) packet frozen
   puff pastry*
4–5 slices Parma ham
1 egg yolk, beaten to glaze

Allow the pastry to thaw at
room temperature for 1 hour.
   Roll out the pastry thinly on
a floured surface and cut into
eight to ten oblongs, measuring
5 × 10 cm/2 × 4 inches. Cut
each slice of ham in half lengthways and roll up. Place a rolled
slice of ham on each piece of
pastry. Brush the edges with
beaten egg yolk, fold over and
press together well. Brush the
surface of the pasties with egg
yolk. Cut very narrow strips of
pastry from the leftover trimmings and place in a cross on
the pasties. Brush with egg
yolk. Preheat the oven to hot
(220°C, 425°F, Gas Mark 7).
   Sprinkle a baking tray with
cold water, place the pasties on

it and leave in the refrigerator
for 15 minutes. Bake near the
top of the oven for 15–20
minutes and serve hot.

Cook's Tip

Instead of rolling the
ham, it can be finely
chopped.

Rich Game
Pasties

*1 (368-g/13-oz) packet frozen
   puff pastry*
1 egg yolk
1 tablespoon milk
FILLING
*350 g/12 oz lean venison or
   pheasant*
100 g/4 oz butter
100 g/4 oz mushrooms
juice of 2 oranges
¼ teaspoon dried marjoram
¼ teaspoon pepper
¼ teaspoon salt
3 tablespoons brandy
4 tablespoons double cream
3 tablespoons chopped parsley

Allow the pastry to thaw at
room temperature for 1 hour.
   Mince the venison or
pheasant and brown in the
butter, stirring continuously.
Wash the mushrooms and chop
them. Add to the meat with the

orange juice, marjoram, pepper
and salt. Leave to cook until
most of the liquid has evapor-
ated. Pour the brandy over the
mixture, heat slightly, flame
and allow to burn out. Leave
the filling to cool then stir in
the double cream and parsley.
   Roll out the pastry to 3 mm/
⅛ inch thick and cut into 12
equal squares. Divide the filling
between the squares, moisten
the edges of the pastry with a
little water and fold over to
enclose the filling. Press down
well to seal. Beat the egg yolk
with the milk and brush the
pasties with this mixture. Place
on a baking tray sprinkled with
cold water and leave in the
refrigerator for 15 minutes.
Preheat the oven to moderately
hot (200°C, 400°F, Gas Mark
6) and bake the pasties towards
the top of the oven for 20–25
minutes. Serve hot.

Pizzas

Bacon Pizza

PIZZA DOUGH
30 g/1 oz fresh yeast
250 ml/8 fl oz lukewarm milk
500 g/1 lb plain flour
pinch of sugar
60 g/2 oz butter
1 egg
¼ teaspoon salt
TOPPING
500 g/1 lb streaky bacon
1 tablespoon caraway seeds
(optional)

Lightly grease two 24-cm/9½-inch flan tins. Cream the yeast with a little of the lukewarm milk. Gradually add all the milk. Sift the flour into a bowl, make a well in the centre and pour in the yeast liquid and sugar. Sprinkle a little of the flour over the liquid and leave to stand in a warm place for 15 minutes, until frothy.

Melt the butter, stir the beaten egg and salt into it then add to the yeast liquid. Gradually mix in all the flour and knead the dough until it is smooth and springy (about 5–10 minutes). Cover and leave to stand in a warm place for 30 minutes.

Cut the bacon into small pieces. Lightly knead the dough then roll out on a floured board and line the flan tins. Spread the bacon pieces over the dough and brush the edges of the pizza with a little oil. Sprinkle with caraway seeds and leave to stand in a warm place for 15 minutes. Preheat the oven to hot (220°C, 425°F, Gas Mark 7). Bake for 25 minutes and serve hot.

Alternatively the dough may be rolled out to line one large baking tray.

Onion Pizza

PIZZA DOUGH
20 g/¾ oz fresh yeast
125 ml/4 fl oz lukewarm milk
300 g/11 oz plain flour
80 g/3 oz butter
1 teaspoon salt
TOPPING
25 g/1 oz butter
100 g/4 oz streaky bacon,
  chopped
1·5 kg/3 lb onions, thinly sliced
150 ml/¼ pint soured cream
2 eggs
pinch of salt
1 tablespoon caraway seeds
  (optional)

Grease a 31-cm/12½-inch square baking tray.

Cream the yeast with a little of the milk. Gradually add the remaining milk. Sift the flour into a bowl and make a well in the centre. Pour the yeast liquid into it and sprinkle with a little of the flour. Cover and leave to stand in a warm place for 15 minutes, until frothy.

Melt the butter and add to the yeast mixture with the salt, then stir in all the flour. Knead the dough until it is smooth and springy (5–10 minutes). Leave the yeast dough to stand in a warm place for 15 minutes. Preheat the oven to moderately hot (200°C, 400°F, Gas Mark 6).

Melt the butter in a frying pan, add the bacon and cook until lightly browned. Add the onion and cook until soft. Roll out the dough on a floured board and line the baking tray. Turn the edges of the dough up to form a rim. Beat the cream with the eggs, salt and caraway seeds. Mix in the onion and bacon and spread the mixture over the pizza dough. Leave to stand in a warm place for a further 15 minutes, then bake for 45 minutes.

Serve hot if possible.

80

Salami Pizza

PIZZA DOUGH
225 g/8 oz plain flour
¼ teaspoon salt
15 g/½ oz fresh yeast
½ teaspoon sugar
150 ml/¼ pint lukewarm milk
2 tablespoons olive oil
TOPPING
6 ripe tomatoes
6 small red chilli peppers
  (optional)
50 g/2 oz Gruyère cheese slices
225 g/8 oz salami, sliced
2 tablespoons olive oil
1 teaspoon dried basil
freshly ground black pepper

Grease two 15-cm/6-inch sand-wich tins with oil.

Sift the flour and salt into a bowl and make a well in the centre. Cream the yeast with the sugar, milk and a little of the flour. Pour into the well in the flour, sprinkle with flour then cover and leave in a warm place for 15 minutes, until frothy.

Gradually work in the rest of the flour with the olive oil and knead for 5–10 minutes. Divide the dough in half and roll out to fit the sandwich tins. Preheat the oven to moderate (180°C, 350°F, Gas Mark 4).

Peel and halve the tomatoes and arrange on the pizza bases with the cut sides uppermost. Cut the stalks off the chilli peppers, halve lengthways and remove seeds. Cut the cheese into 1-cm/½-inch wide strips. Arrange the chillis, strips of cheese and slices of salami between and over the tomatoes. Sprinkle with the oil, basil and freshly ground black pepper. Leave the pizzas for a further 15 minutes. Bake near the top of the oven for 40 minutes and serve hot.

Note The red chilli peppers may be too hot for some tastes.

Neapolitan Pizza

PIZZA DOUGH
225 g/8 oz plain flour
¼ teaspoon salt
15 g/½ oz fresh yeast
½ teaspoon sugar
150 ml/¼ pint lukewarm milk
2 tablespoons olive oil
TOPPING
4 tomatoes
1 teaspoon celery salt
1 teaspoon black pepper
2 teaspoons dried oregano
100 g/4 oz Mozzarella cheese
2 onions, chopped
10 anchovy fillets
1 tablespoon capers
2 tablespoons olive oil

Sift the flour and salt into a bowl and make a well in the centre. Cream the yeast with the sugar, milk and a little of the flour. Pour into the well, sprinkle with flour then cover and leave in a warm place for 15 minutes, until frothy.

Gradually work in the rest of the flour with the olive oil and knead the dough for 5–10 minutes. Roll out thinly into two 18-cm/7-inch rounds. Place on a greased baking tray and turn up the edges slightly. Preheat the oven to moderate (180°C, 350°F, Gas Mark 4).

Peel and slice the tomatoes and place on the pizzas. Add the celery salt, pepper, oregano and slices of cheese. Scatter over the onions, anchovies and capers. Sprinkle with the oil and leave the pizzas for 15 minutes. Bake near the top of the oven for 40 minutes and serve hot.

Spicy Flans

Mushroom and Cheese Flan

PASTRY
250 g/9 oz plain flour
125 g/4½ oz butter or margarine,
  cut into flakes
¼ teaspoon salt
2–3 tablespoons water
1 egg yolk
FILLING
1 leek
150 g/5 oz ham
225 g/8 oz button mushrooms
100 g/4 oz Camembert cheese
10 stuffed green olives
2 tablespoons oil
20 g/¾ oz butter
20 g/¾ oz plain flour
300 ml/½ pint milk
2 tablespoons chopped mixed
  herbs
¼ teaspoon each salt and pepper
1 egg yolk

Place the sifted flour in a mixing bowl with the butter or
margarine, salt, water and egg
yolk, and mix until a pastry
dough is formed. Cover and
leave for 2 hours in the
refrigerator.
　Trim and wash the leek. Dice
the ham, leek, mushrooms and
Camembert and slice the olives.
Heat the oil and brown the
diced ham. Add the leek and
mushrooms and simmer for a
further 10 minutes.
　Melt the butter, cook the
flour lightly in it, pour in the
milk and bring to the boil, stirring continuously. Stir the
herbs, seasoning, beaten egg
yolk and diced Camembert
into this sauce. Preheat the
oven to hot (220°C, 425°F, Gas
Mark 7).
　Roll out the pastry to line a
25-cm/10-inch flan tin. Spread
the mushroom filling over the
base, pour on the sauce and
sprinkle with the olives. Bake
for 40–50 minutes and serve
hot.

Country Leek Flan

PASTRY
200 g/7 oz plain flour
pinch of salt
1 egg
1–2 tablespoons water
100 g/3½ oz butter or margarine,
  cut into flakes
FILLING
450 g/1 lb leeks
175 g/6 oz streaky bacon
1 tablespoon oil
salt and freshly ground black
  pepper
pinch of curry powder
225 g/8 oz pork breakfast
  sausage, sliced
2 eggs
250 ml/8 fl oz soured cream

Place the sifted flour in a mixing bowl with the salt, egg,
water and butter, and mix until
a pastry dough is formed.
Cover and leave for 2 hours in
the refrigerator.
　Trim, wash and slice the
leeks. Dice the bacon and
brown in the oil. Add the
leeks, sprinkle with a pinch of
salt, pepper and curry powder
and cook gently for 10 minutes.
Preheat the oven to moderately
hot (200°C, 400°F, Gas Mark
6).
　Roll out the pastry to line a
23-cm/9-inch flan tin. Prick the
base several times with a fork.
Remove the rind from the
breakfast sausage and lay the
slices over the pastry base.
Spread with the leek filling.
Beat the eggs with the soured
cream and seasoning to taste
and pour over the filling. Bake
for 50–60 minutes and serve
hot from the tin.

Piquant Cheese Flan

1 (368-g/13-oz) packet frozen
  puff pastry
FILLING
150 g/5 oz ham
450 g/1 lb cream cheese
1 tablespoon tomato purée
1 tablespoon paprika pepper
pinch each of salt, white pepper
  and sugar
few drops of Worcestershire
  sauce
1 small clove garlic
3 tablespoons chopped mixed
  herbs
12 small red chilli peppers
  (optional)
12 capers

Allow the puff pastry to thaw
for 1 hour at room temperature. Divide in half and roll out
each half into a 20-cm/8-inch
round. Sprinkle a baking tray
with cold water, place the

pastry rounds on it, prick
lightly with a fork and leave to
stand for 15 minutes.

Preheat the oven to hot
(220°C, 425°F, Gas Mark 7)
and bake the pastry near the
top of the oven for 10–15
minutes.

Finely chop the ham and mix
with half the cream cheese, the
tomato purée and paprika.
Season with salt, pepper, sugar
and Worcestershire sauce.
Crush the garlic and mix with
150 g/5 oz cream cheese, the
herbs and a little seasoning.
Beat the rest of the cream
cheese to soften it for piping.
Cover one pastry base with the
tomato, ham and cream cheese
mixture, place the second round
of pastry on top and cover with
the cream cheese containing the
herbs. Mark into twelve using
the blade of a knife. Decorate
the top with swirls of piped
cream cheese, topped with the
red chillis and capers.

Prawn and Artichoke Flan

1 (212-g/7½-oz) packet frozen
  puff pastry
TOPPING
100 g/4 oz frozen prawns
1 (200-g/7-oz) can artichoke
  hearts, drained
20 stuffed green olives
½ (184-g/6½-oz) can pimientos
1 (300-ml/½-pint) packet aspic
mayonnaise
2 tablespoons wholemeal
  breadcrumbs
2 eggs, hard-boiled
2 tablespoons caviar or lumpfish
  roe

Allow the pastry and the
prawns to thaw for 1 hour at
room temperature.

Preheat the oven to hot
(220°C, 425°F, Gas Mark 7).
Roll the pastry out to line the
base of a 25-cm/10-inch flan
ring and leave in the refrigera-

tor for 15 minutes. Prick the
pastry all over with a fork and
bake towards the top of the
oven for 15 minutes. Leave to
cool.

Quarter the artichoke hearts,
slice the olives and cut the
pimientos into strips. Arrange
these ingredients over the
pastry base with the prawns.
Make up the aspic according to
the instructions on the packet.
When on the point of setting
pour over the flan and leave to
set. Remove the flan ring,
spread the sides with a little
mayonnaise and sprinkle with
the breadcrumbs. Garnish with
swirls of mayonnaise, quartered
eggs and caviar.

Celebration Cakes

Chocolate Hedgehogs

SHORTBREAD BASE
100 g/3½ oz butter, cut into flakes
60 g/2 oz castor sugar
pinch of salt
160 g/5½ oz plain flour
TOPPING
1 (600-ml/1-pint) packet vanilla blancmange powder
450 ml/¾ pint milk
2 egg yolks
100 g/4 oz sugar
40 g/1½ oz cocoa powder
5 tablespoons boiling water
250 g/9 oz butter
1 sponge or sandwich cake (see page 228; use half quantities)
6 tablespoons water
DECORATION
100 g/4 oz blanched almonds, cut into quarters lengthways
350 g/12 oz plain chocolate

Knead the butter, sugar, salt and sifted flour together to give a firm, smooth dough. Wrap in foil or cling film and leave for 2 hours in the refrigerator.

Cut a cardboard pattern in the shape of a pointed oval, 8–9 cm/3½ inches long. Preheat the oven to moderately hot (200°C, 400°F, Gas Mark 6).

Roll out the shortbread to 5 mm/¼ inch thick and, using the cardboard pattern, cut out hedgehog-shaped pieces. Arrange on greased baking trays and bake for 10–12 minutes. Leave to cool on the baking trays for a minute then remove to a wire rack to cool completely.

Mix the blancmange powder to a smooth cream with 3 tablespoons milk and whisk in the egg yolks. Bring the rest of the milk to the boil with half the sugar. Pour into the blended blancmange powder, stir well and return to the saucepan. Bring to the boil, stirring con-

tinuously, and cook for 1 minute until thick and smooth. Leave to cool, stirring occasionally to prevent a skin forming. Reserve 3 tablespoons of the blancmange to make the hedgehog eyes and noses. Cream the cocoa powder with the boiling water and beat into the blancmange. Cream the butter until soft and light. When the blancmange is cool, gradually beat the butter into it until smooth.

Cut the sponge or sandwich cake into 1-cm/½-inch cubes and place in a bowl. Dissolve the remaining sugar in the water and bring to the boil. Pour over the cake cubes, cover and leave for 30 minutes. Mix the cake cubes carefully into the chocolate mixture and chill in the refrigerator for 1 hour. When firm, pile this chocolate mixture on the shortbread bases to form a hedgehog shape, and smooth over with a knife. Stick the almond quar-

ters into the hedgehogs all over but leave the heads as they are. Place the hedgehogs in the refrigerator for 1 hour to become firm.

Melt the chocolate in a basin over a pan of hot water. Stand the hedgehogs on greaseproof paper and coat them completely with the chocolate. Make noses and eyes from the reserved blancmange, as illustrated.

Chocolate Faces

CAKE MIXTURE
4 eggs, separated, plus 2 egg
*   whites*
120 g/4½ oz castor sugar
grated rind of ¼ lemon
1 tablespoon water
50 g/2 oz plain flour
60 g/2½ oz cornflour
ICING AND DECORATION
100 g/4 oz apricot jam
100 g/4 oz plain chocolate
1 egg white
50 g/2 oz icing sugar
1 tube Smarties

Line a baking tray with non-
stick baking parchment. Preheat the oven to moderate
(180°C, 350°F, Gas Mark 4).

Beat the egg yolks with 25 g/
1 oz sugar, the lemon rind and
water until frothy. Whisk the
egg whites until stiff, whisk in
the remaining sugar and fold
into the egg yolk mixture. Sift
over the flour and cornflour

and fold in well. Turn this mixture into a piping bag fitted
with a large plain nozzle and
pipe quite large half-spheres on
to the non-stick paper. Bake
for 12–15 minutes then leave
to cool on a wire rack.

Remove the paper and stick
two halves together with a little
jam. Melt the chocolate in a
basin over hot water and use to
cover the cakes. Add sufficient
lightly whisked egg white to the
sifted icing sugar until the icing
is of a piping consistency. Pipe
faces on to the cakes, as illustrated, using coloured Smarties
to represent the eyes.

Alphabet Biscuits

180 g/6 oz plain flour
1 egg
90 g/3 oz castor sugar
25 g/1 oz vanilla sugar
60 g/2 oz butter, cut into flakes
ICING
200 g/7 oz icing sugar
2–3 tablespoons lemon juice
50 g/2 oz jelly bears

Sift the flour on to a pastry
board and knead to a dough
with the egg, sugar, vanilla
sugar and butter. Wrap in
foil or cling film and leave for
2 hours in the refrigerator.

Preheat the oven to
moderately hot (200°C, 400°F,
Gas Mark 6). Cut small pieces
from the biscuit dough and
form into sausage shapes
about 1 cm/½ inch in diameter.
Make a letter from each
sausage and flatten slightly.

Place on a greased baking
tray and bake in the centre of
the oven for 8–10 minutes.

Stir the sifted icing sugar
with enough lemon juice to
give a thick icing, but thin
enough to spread. Ice the
letters with it while still warm
and stick the jelly bears on to
the icing before it sets.

Cook's Tip

When you are making
the letters for older
children or adults, use
candied coffee beans for
the decoration.

Chocolate Ice Waffles

WAFFLE BATTER
60 g/2 oz butter
25 g/1 oz castor sugar
1 tablespoon vanilla sugar
pinch of salt
2 eggs
125 g/4 oz plain flour
¼ teaspoon baking powder
175 ml/6 fl oz buttermilk
FILLING AND TOPPING
150 ml/¼ pint double cream
1 tablespoon castor sugar
100 g/4 oz plain chocolate
1 (483-ml/17-fl oz) block chocolate ripple ice cream
20 g/¾ oz pistachio nuts, chopped

Beat the butter with the sugar, vanilla sugar and salt until pale and creamy. Beat in the eggs one at a time then add the sifted flour and baking powder. Mix in the buttermilk

to give a thick batter. Heat the waffle iron and brush lightly with melted butter. Cook the waffles individually until golden brown.

Whip the cream with the sugar until stiff and use to fill a piping bag fitted with a star nozzle. Melt the chocolate in a basin over a pan of hot water and allow to cool but not set. Just before serving, place a wedge of ice cream on half the waffles and cover each with a second waffle. Decorate as illustrated with rosettes of piped cream, chocolate icing and chopped pistachios.

Ice Cream Roll

SPONGE MIXTURE
4 eggs, separated, plus 2 egg yolks
100 g/4 oz castor sugar
80 g/3 oz plain flour
20 g/1 oz cornflour
FILLING
350 g/12 oz orange jelly marmalade
150 ml/¼ pint double cream
1 tablespoon castor sugar
1 (483-ml/17-fl oz) block Neapolitan ice cream

Line a 34 × 24-cm/13½ × 9½-inch Swiss roll tin with greased greaseproof paper. Preheat the oven to hot (220°C, 425°F, Gas Mark 7).

Beat all the egg yolks with half the sugar until pale and creamy. Whisk the egg whites until stiff, slowly add the rest of the sugar and whisk until smooth and glossy. Fold into the egg yolks. Sift the flour

and cornflour together and fold carefully into the egg mixture. Spread evenly into the tin and bake for 10–12 minutes.

Turn out, while still hot, on to a tea towel sprinkled with castor sugar. Remove the lining paper and trim the edges of the cake. Sieve the marmalade and spread it evenly over the cake. With the help of the tea towel, roll the cake up firmly and cool on a wire rack. Whip the cream and sugar until stiff and place in a piping bag fitted with a star nozzle.

When the roll is cool, cut into 1-cm/½-inch slices and sandwich a 1-cm/½-inch slice of ice cream between each pair of slices until both roll and ice cream are used up. Decorate with rosettes of cream.

Coffee Meringue Kisses

MERINGUE
1¼ tablespoons instant coffee
  powder
8 egg whites
200 g/7 oz castor sugar
150 g/5 oz icing sugar
30 g/1 oz cornflour
FILLING
2 teaspoons cornflour
1 (213-g/7½-oz) can cherries
50 g/2 oz sugar
¼ teaspoon ground cinnamon
300 ml/½ pint double cream
1 tablespoon castor sugar

Dissolve the coffee powder in just enough hot water to blend it. Allow to cool. Line two baking trays with non-stick baking parchment or grease-proof paper. (If using the latter, grease lightly.) Preheat the oven to very cool (120°C, 250°F, Gas Mark ½).

Whisk the egg whites until stiff and slowly add the castor sugar, whisking continuously. Sift the icing sugar and corn-flour on to the egg whites and fold in together with the blended coffee. Fill a piping bag fitted with a star nozzle with the meringue mixture and pipe rosettes on to the baking trays. Bake for 3–4 hours with the door slightly open. Remove from the trays and strip off the paper.

Blend the cornflour with a little of the drained cherry juice. Bring the rest of the cherry juice to the boil with the sugar and cinnamon, add the blended cornflour and stir until thickened. Add the stoned cherries, bring back to the boil then leave to cool.

Whip the cream with the sugar. Pipe a ring of cream on to the flat side of half the meringues, fill the centre with the cherry sauce and place a second meringue on top.

Banana Meringues

MERINGUE
4 egg whites
100 g/3½ oz castor sugar
70 g/2¾ oz icing sugar
15 g/½ oz cornflour
FILLING AND TOPPING
300 ml/½ pint double cream
3 tablespoons icing sugar
1 tablespoon cocoa powder
100 g/4 oz plain chocolate
6 bananas
50 g/2 oz soft brown sugar

Line a baking tray with non-stick baking parchment or greaseproof paper. (If using the latter, grease lightly.) Preheat the oven to very cool (120°C, 250°F, Gas Mark ½).

Whisk the egg whites until stiff then slowly add the castor sugar, whisking continuously. Sift over the icing sugar and cornflour and fold in. Fill a piping bag fitted with a plain nozzle with the meringue mixture and pipe 12 banana shapes on to the prepared baking tray. Bake for 3–4 hours with the oven door slightly open.

Remove the meringues from the baking tray and peel off the paper. Leave to cool.

Whip the cream with the sifted icing sugar until stiff then stir in the sifted cocoa powder. Using a star nozzle, pipe this cocoa cream on to the meringues. Melt the chocolate in a basin over a pan of hot water and allow to cool slightly. Peel the bananas and cut in half lengthways. Place a halved banana on each cream-topped meringue and pour over the chocolate icing. Sprinkle with brown sugar before the icing sets.

Wedding Cakes

Traditional Wedding Cake

CAKE MIXTURE
250 g/9 oz butter
250 g/9 oz castor sugar
5 eggs
grated rind and juice of 1 lemon
1 tablespoon rum
250 g/9 oz plain flour
¼ teaspoon ground cinnamon
generous pinch of grated
    nutmeg
150 g/5 oz glacé cherries
    washed, dried and roughly
    chopped
400 g/14 oz currants
400 g/14 oz raisins
200 g/7 oz chopped mixed peel
50 g/2 oz blanched almonds,
    chopped
ROYAL ICING
3 large egg whites
675 g/1½ lb icing sugar
1 teaspoon lemon juice
sugar flowers to decorate

Grease a 25-cm/10-inch cake tin with butter or margarine. Line the greased tin with greaseproof paper and grease this thoroughly. Preheat the oven to cool (140°C, 275°F, Gas Mark 1).

Beat the butter with the sugar until pale and creamy. Beat in the eggs one at a time with the lemon rind and juice and the rum. Add a little flour if necessary to prevent the mixture curdling. Sift the remaining flour and mix with the cinnamon, nutmeg, cherries, currants, raisins, chopped peel and almonds. Add to the creamed mixture, folding it all in thoroughly. Pour into the cake tin and smooth the surface. Wrap a double thickness of brown paper or newspaper around the tin and secure it with string. This will prevent the outside of the cake from becoming overcooked before the middle is cooked through.

Bake the cake for 4½–5½ hours. It is essential to test with a skewer (see page 225) before removing the cake from the oven. If necessary continue baking for a little longer. Leave to cool for a short while in the tin then turn out on to a wire rack.

Lightly whisk the egg whites and brush a little over the surface of the cake. Gradually beat the sifted icing sugar and lemon juice into the remaining egg white to give a firm icing. Ice the top and sides of the cake, spreading smoothly with a palette knife. Place the rest of the icing in a piping bag fitted with a small star nozzle and decorate as illustrated.

Note To make the variation on the jacket, bake the cake mixture in a 25-cm/10-inch round fluted cake tin. When cool, brush over a very thin glacé icing and decorate with candied fruits and angelica.

Cook's Tip

The wedding cake will taste best if baked at least 3–4 weeks before the wedding and kept well wrapped in foil. Ice and decorate it just before using.

If well wrapped, the cake will keep for up to 1 year. In England it is customary in many families to make a two or three-tier wedding cake and to keep the second tier for the christening of the first child.

The traditional wedding cake is often covered with a layer of almond paste before the royal icing; this gives a smoother surface on which to ice.

96

Wedding Cakes

Three-Tier Wedding Cake

For this wedding cake you will need twice the ingredients given in the recipe for Traditional Wedding Cake (left)

DECORATION
coloured sugar balls, crystallised violets, glacé cherries, angelica and round wafer biscuits

Generously grease and line with greased greaseproof paper three 25-cm/10-inch, 18-cm/7-inch, 13-cm/5-inch cake tins. Preheat the oven to cool (140°C, 275°F, Gas Mark 1) and prepare the cake mixture as in the preceding recipe. Bake the cakes, checking the smallest after 2½–3 hours and the middle size after 3-4 hours. Before removing from the oven test each of the cakes with a skewer (see page 225) and if necessary bake for a little longer.

Leave to cool on a wire rack, wrap in foil and keep for 3-4 weeks.

Lightly whisk the egg whites and brush over the surface of the cakes. Sift the icing sugar and mix to a firm icing with the lemon juice and the remaining egg whites. Cover the top and sides of all three cakes with the icing and when completely set place one upon the other.

Place the rest of the icing in a piping bag fitted with a small star nozzle and in a small greaseproof paper piping bag. Using the illustration as a guide, decorate the cake with piped icing, sugar balls, glacé cherries, crystallised violets and angelica. Cut some of the wafer biscuits into quarters, cover thinly with icing and use to decorate the cake as illustrated. Place three iced wafers on top of the cake to form a crown and decorate.

Fleurons

*1 (368-g/13-oz) packet frozen
puff pastry
1 egg yolk, beaten to glaze*

Allow the pastry to thaw for
1 hour at room temperature.
Roll out the pastry to
5 mm/¼ inch thick. With a
round pastry cutter or a glass,
cut half-moon shapes from
the pastry, starting at the edge.
Place the remains of the pastry
in a pile, press firmly together,
roll out and cut more half-
moons. Sprinkle a baking tray
with cold water, place the
half-moons on it and brush
with egg yolk. Lightly mark a
lattice pattern on top of each
with a knife and chill in the
refrigerator for 15 minutes.
Preheat the oven to hot
(220°C, 425°F, Gas Mark 7).
Bake the fleurons for 15
minutes towards the top of the
oven and serve warm.

Cook's Tip

Fleurons can be served to
accompany a special
soup or to garnish a
particularly delicious fish
dish.

Cheese Twists

*1 (368-g/13-oz) packet frozen
puff pastry
1 egg
salt and pepper
50 g/2 oz Emmenthal cheese,
finely grated*

Allow the pastry to thaw at
room temperature for 1 hour.
Divide the pastry into thirds
and roll each piece out to give
an oblong of 35 × 13 cm /
14 × 5 inches. Brush each
piece of pastry generously with
the seasoned, beaten egg and
sandwich the three pieces
together with the cheese. Press
together well and cut into thin
strips measuring approxi-
mately 5 mm/¼ inch wide.
Twist the strips and place on
baking trays which have been
sprinkled with cold water.
Leave to stand in a cool place
for 15 minutes.
Preheat the oven to moderately hot (200°C, 400°F, Gas
Mark 6) and bake the cheese
twists for 15 minutes. Serve at
once if possible.

Cook's Tip

When baking puff
pastry, always sprinkle
the baking tray or tin
with cold water before
beginning. The steam
from the water helps the
pastry to rise.

American Muffins

250 ml/8 fl oz milk
50 g/2 oz cornmeal
30 g/1 oz self-raising flour
2 teaspoons baking powder
1 teaspoon salt
2 teaspoons sugar
1 egg
50 g/2 oz butter, softened

Grease 10–12 patty tins with butter or margarine. Preheat the oven to moderately hot (200°C, 400°F, Gas Mark 6).

Bring the milk to the boil, sprinkle the cornmeal into it and cook, stirring, for a few minutes, until the mixture leaves the sides of the pan. Sift the flour and baking powder into the mixture and stir in with the salt, sugar, egg and softened butter. Three-quarters fill the prepared tins and bake for 20–30 minutes.

Remove from the tins immediately and serve hot with butter.

Cook's Tip

These American muffins are served at a celebration meal in place of ordinary white bread rolls.

Anchovy Bites

1 (368-g/13-oz) packet frozen puff pastry
1 (56-g/2 oz) can anchovy fillets
1 egg yolk, beaten to glaze
1–2 tablespoons sea salt

Allow the pastry to thaw for 1 hour at room temperature. Roll out on a floured board to 5 mm/¼ inch thick and cut into 6-cm/2½-inch rounds with a fluted cutter. Place a halved anchovy fillet on half the pastry rounds. Brush the edges of each round with egg yolk and sandwich together in pairs, sealing the edges well. Brush the tops with egg yolk and sprinkle with the salt.

Sprinkle a baking tray with cold water, arrange the pastry rounds on it and chill in the refrigerator for 15 minutes. Preheat the oven to hot (220°C, 425°F, Gas Mark 7) and bake towards the top of the oven for 10–15 minutes.

These are best eaten while still warm.

Cook's Tip

Sardines can be used instead of anchovies for the filling.

Vol au Vent Pastry Case

1 (368-g/13-oz) packet frozen
puff pastry
1 egg, beaten

Allow the pastry to thaw at room temperature for about 1 hour. Line a 1·5-litre/2½-pint pudding basin with foil. Fill with crumpled absorbent paper, pressing down lightly. Fold the foil over and lightly secure. Turn out this foil mould. Sprinkle a large baking tray with cold water and pre-heat the oven to hot (220°C, 425°F, Gas Mark 7).

Roll out the pastry to a rectangle approximately 50 × 30 cm / 20 × 12 inches. Cut out a round measuring approximately 19 cm / 7½ inches in diameter and place on the baking tray. Stand the foil mould in the middle of this pastry round, with the narrow end at the top. Cut out another pastry round large enough to cover the mould (approximately 33 cm/13 inches in diameter). Brush the edges of both pastry rounds with beaten egg. Carefully place the large round of pastry over the foil mould and seal the edges to the pastry base. Flute the edges with a knife, as illustrated, and brush all over with beaten egg. Cut out shapes from the remaining pastry trimmings and use to decorate the pastry case. Glaze these with beaten egg and bake the vol au vent for 15–20 minutes.

Remove from the oven and, using a sharp pointed knife, cut a round lid from the top of the pastry case. Remove this lid carefully and cut a hole in the foil underneath. Carefully remove the absorbent paper then crumple the foil and remove this also from the pastry shell. Fill and serve immediately if required warm, or allow to cool and then fill.

Cook's Tip

The vol au vent case can be filled with a hot chicken, veal or mush-room mixture, with cold lobster cocktail or with a crab and prawn mousse. For a dessert, fill with a sweet custard or cream.

The vol au vent case can be reheated success-fully if you wish to make it in advance and still serve it hot. Heat the filling separately and fill the case just before serv-ing, or heat the vol au vent case already filled.

Hot or cold, sweet or savoury, this vol au vent makes a spectacular buffet party dish.

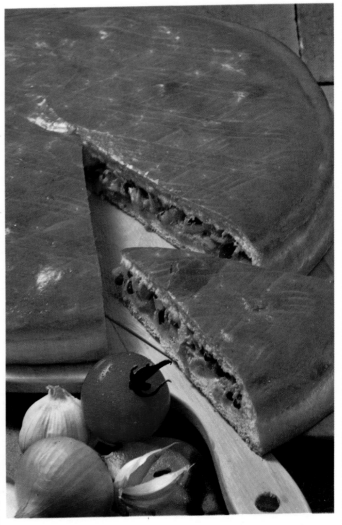

Royal
Vols aux Vent

1 (368-g/13-oz) packet frozen
*   puff pastry*
1 egg yolk, beaten to glaze

To make these vols aux vent
you will need two sharp pastry
cutters: one 6 cm/2½ inches in
diameter and one 3·5 cm/1½
inches in diameter.

Allow the pastry to thaw at
room temperature for 1 hour.

Roll the pastry out to 5 mm/
¼ inch thick. Cut out an even
number of rounds using the
6-cm/2½-inch cutter. Cut out
the centre of half the rounds
using the 3·5-cm/1½-inch
cutter. Brush the rounds with
water and place the rings on
top then lightly mark a circle
inside the hole with a pointed
knife. Brush with beaten egg
yolk and leave in the refrigerator for 30 minutes. Preheat the
oven to hot (220°C, 425°F,
Gas Mark 7).

Bake for 15–20 minutes
then cool on a wire rack and
fill according to taste.

Cook's Tip

Prepare a chicken filling
for the vols aux vent as
illustrated. Make up a
thick white sauce, using
half chicken stock and
half milk. Fold in diced
cooked chicken and
frozen green peas,
heating through com-
pletely. Season to taste
and spoon into the vol au
vent cases.

Basque Chicken
Pie

500 g/1 lb risen white bread
*   dough, made with 500 g/1 lb*
*   flour, etc. (see page 226)*
1 egg, beaten to glaze
FILLING
1 red pepper
1 green pepper
1 large onion
225 g/8 oz tomatoes
50 g/2 oz ham
350 g/12 oz cooked chicken
2 tablespoons oil
¼ clove garlic, crushed
1 teaspoon salt
¼ teaspoon pepper

Preheat the oven to moderately hot (200°C, 400°F, Gas
Mark 6).

First prepare the filling.
Remove cores, pith and seeds
from the peppers, then chop
finely. Peel and chop the onion
and tomatoes. Dice the meats.

Heat the oil and fry the
peppers, onion and garlic
gently for 10 minutes. Add the
tomatoes, ham and chicken
and bring to a simmer. Stir in
the salt and pepper and remove
from the heat.

Divide the bread dough in
half and roll out on a floured
surface into two rounds, each
about 30 cm/12 inches in
diameter. Place one round on a
greased baking tray. Spread
over the chicken mixture to
within 1 cm/½ inch of the edge.
Place the second round on top
and press the edges together to
seal. Score with a knife, brush
with the beaten egg and bake
for 45 minutes.

Desserts with a Difference

Raspberry Ice Cream Cake

SPONGE MIXTURE
3 eggs
65 g/2¼ oz castor sugar
pinch of salt
50 g/2 oz plain flour
25 g/1 oz cornflour
25 g/1 oz ground almonds
25 g/1 oz butter, melted
FILLING AND TOPPING
1 tablespoon Kirsch
225 g/8 oz raspberries
600 ml/1 pint double cream
250 g/9 oz castor sugar
chocolate caraque (see page 231)

Grease and flour a 20-cm/8-inch cake tin. Preheat the oven to moderately hot (190°C, 375°F, Gas Mark 5).

Beat the eggs with the sugar and salt until pale and creamy. Sift the flour with the cornflour and fold into the mixture with the ground almonds and butter.

Place in the cake tin and bake for 25–30 minutes.

Turn on to a wire rack to cool for 24 hours then cut into two layers. Line the sides of the cake tin with foil and place one of the layers over the base.

Spoon the Kirsch over the raspberries, cover and leave for 1 hour. Keep a few whole raspberries for decoration and crush the remainder lightly.

Whip the cream with the sugar until stiff. Reserve approximately a quarter of this cream and stir the raspberries into the remainder. Pour into the cake tin and place the second cake layer on top. Freeze for 5–10 hours in a freezer or in the freezing compartment of a refrigerator.

Leave at room temperature for 15 minutes then turn out. Spread a little of the reserved cream thinly over the top and sides of the cake and decorate as illustrated.

Hazelnut Ice Cream Cake

SPONGE MIXTURE
3 eggs
65 g/2¼ oz castor sugar
25 g/1 oz plain flour
30 g/1 oz cornflour
75 g/3 oz toasted hazelnuts,
  finely ground
FILLING AND TOPPING
600 ml/1 pint double cream
225 g/8 oz castor sugar
75 g/3 oz toasted hazelnuts,
  ground
few whole hazelnuts

Grease and flour a 20-cm/8-inch cake tin. Preheat the oven to moderately hot (190°C, 375°F, Gas Mark 5).

Whisk the eggs with the sugar until pale and creamy. Sift the flour with the corn-flour and carefully fold in with the ground hazelnuts. Pour into the cake tin and bake for 25–30 minutes.

Turn on to a wire rack to cool. Leave the cake for 24 hours then cut it through into two layers. Line the sides of the cake tin with foil and place one of the layers over the base.

Whip the cream with the sugar until stiff. Reserve a third of this cream then add 50 g/2 oz ground hazelnuts to the remainder. Spread over the cake base and place the second cake layer on top. Freeze the cake for 5–10 hours in the freezer or in the freezing compartment of the refrigerator.

Leave at room temperature for 15 minutes then turn out and decorate. Use a little of the reserved cream to spread thinly over the top and sides of the cake then sprinkle with the remaining grounds nuts. With the rest of the cream, pipe rosettes on the cake and top these with whole hazelnuts. Serve at once.

Desserts with a Difference

Baked Alaska

SPONGE BASE
1 egg
25 g/1 oz castor sugar
25 g/1 oz plain flour
TOPPING
50 g/2 oz ground almonds
50 g/2 oz apricot jam
1 tablespoon rum
50 g/2 oz candied lemon peel
4 egg whites
225 g/8 oz castor sugar
1 block each raspberry ripple
   and raspberry ice cream
8 glacé cherries
2 teaspoons flaked almonds

Preheat the oven to 190°C, 375°F, Gas Mark 5. Grease and flour a 15-cm/6-inch sandwich tin. Whisk the egg with the sugar until pale. Fold in the sifted flour and turn into the tin. Bake for 20–25 minutes then cool.

Mix the ground almonds with the jam, rum and chopped peel. Whisk the egg whites until stiff, fold in the sugar and place in a piping bag.

Spread the almond mixture over the cake base. Place the raspberry ripple ice cream on the centre and surround with the raspberry ice cream cut into pieces. Smooth over. Place in a freezer for 30 minutes until firm. Preheat the oven to 240°C, 475°F, Gas Mark 9.

Cover the cake completely with the whisked egg white, decorate with glacé cherries and flaked almonds and brown in the oven for 3–4 minutes. Serve at once.

Baked Chocolate Alaska

Make a sponge base as above, using twice the quantity of ingredients, and bake in a 15 × 23-cm/6 × 9-inch shallow tin. Trim to fit a block of Neapolitan ice cream, spread with 2 tablespoons redcurrant jelly and place the ice cream on top. Whisk 4 egg whites with 225 g/8 oz castor sugar as above, adding 1 teaspoon sifted cocoa powder. Pipe all over and brown in a very hot oven (240°C, 475°F, Gas Mark 9) for 3–4 minutes. Sift over chocolate powder before serving at once.

Cherry Meringue Nests

MERINGUE
6 egg whites
225 g/8 oz castor sugar
75 g/3 oz icing sugar
30 g/1 oz cornflour
TOPPING
1 tablespoon instant coffee
  powder
250 ml/8 fl oz double cream
2 tablespoons castor sugar
1 (425-g/15-oz) can red
  cherries
1 (483-ml/17-fl oz) block
  vanilla ice cream

Line a baking tray with non-stick baking parchment or lightly greased greaseproof paper. Preheat the oven to very cool (110°C, 225°F, Gas Mark ¼).

Whisk the egg whites until stiff then whisk in the castor sugar until stiff and glossy.

Fold in the sifted icing sugar and cornflour. Fill a piping bag fitted with a star nozzle with the meringue mixture and pipe rosette shapes on to the baking tray. Leave to dry out in the oven with the door slightly open for 3–4 hours.

Dissolve the coffee powder in 1 tablespoon boiling water and leave to cool. Whip the cream with the sugar until stiff and stir in the coffee. Pipe rings of coffee cream on to the meringue nests. Drain the cherries and pat dry. Place a few cherries in the coffee cream, top with a scoop of ice cream and decorate with the rest of the cherries. Serve at once.

Orange Cream Tartlets

PASTRY
200 g/8 oz plain flour
100 g/4 oz icing sugar
100 g/4 oz butter
2 egg yolks
few drops of vanilla essence
pinch of salt
1 tablespoon water
FILLING AND TOPPING
1 (178-ml/6¼-fl oz) can frozen
  concentrated orange juice
3 tablespoons white wine
100 g/4 oz castor sugar
15 g/½ oz powdered gelatine
300 ml/½ pint double cream
50 g/2 oz drinking chocolate
  powder
1 (483-ml/17-fl oz) block
  raspberry ice cream
50 g/2 oz toasted flaked
  almonds

Sift the flour and icing sugar into a bowl and work in the butter, egg yolks, vanilla essence, salt and water, to make a firm dough. Cover and refrigerate for 2 hours.

Preheat the oven to moderately hot (200°C, 400°F, Gas Mark 6). Roll out the pastry thinly and use to line twelve 7·5-cm/3-inch tartlet tins. Bake blind for 10 minutes, remove the cases from the tins and cool on a wire rack.

Heat the orange juice with the wine and sugar, add the gelatine and warm gently to dissolve it. Leave to cool then place in the refrigerator. Whip the cream until it stands in peaks. As the jelly begins to set, fold in half the cream. Use to fill the tartlet cases and leave to set completely.

Mix the remaining cream with the sifted drinking chocolate powder. Just before serving, place a slice of ice cream on each tartlet, pipe a chocolate cream rosette and sprinkle with almonds.

Desserts with a Difference

Strawberry Cream Puffs

CHOUX PASTE
125 ml/4 fl oz water
30 g/1 oz butter
pinch of salt
95 g/3¼ oz plain flour
2 eggs, beaten
FILLING
225 g/8 oz frozen strawberries
2 tablespoons castor sugar
1 tablespoon rum
150 ml/¼ pint double cream
3 tablespoons icing sugar
1 (483-ml/17-fl oz) block strawberry ice cream

Mix the strawberries with the castor sugar and rum and leave to defrost. Preheat the oven to hot (220°C, 425°F, Gas Mark 7).

Place the water, butter and salt in a saucepan and heat gently until the butter has melted. Bring quickly to the

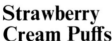

boil then remove from the heat. Add the sifted flour all at once and beat vigorously until the dough forms a ball and comes away from the sides of the pan clean. Return to the heat and cook for 1 minute, stirring all the time. Allow to cool slightly then beat in the eggs a little at a time. Fill a piping bag fitted with a large fluted nozzle with the paste and pipe 16 small rosettes on to a greased baking tray. Bake the rosettes for 20 minutes until puffed and golden.

Cut a lid from each of the choux puffs then leave to cool. Fill the bottom half of the puffs with the soaked strawberries. Whip the cream stiffly with 1 tablespoon sifted icing sugar. With a shallow spoon cut scoops of ice cream and place on the strawberries. Pipe cream on to the ice cream, top with the lids and sift the remaining icing sugar over the top. Serve at once.

Exotic Fruit Meringues

6 egg whites
100 g/4 oz castor sugar
100 g/4 oz icing sugar
30 g/1 oz cornflour
40 g/1½ oz cocoa powder
250 ml/8 fl oz double cream
2 tablespoons icing sugar
6 Chinese gooseberries
1 (483-ml/17-fl oz) block ice cream (flavour of your choice)

Line a baking tray with greased greaseproof paper or non-stick baking parchment. Preheat the oven to very cool (110°C, 225°F, Gas Mark ¼).

Whisk the egg whites until stiff then whisk in the castor sugar. Sift the icing sugar with the cornflour and cocoa powder and fold into the whisked egg whites. Place in a piping bag fitted with a plain nozzle and

pipe 14 oval meringues on to the baking tray.

Leave the meringues to dry out overnight in the centre of the oven, keeping the door slightly ajar with a wooden spoon.

Whip the cream with the sifted icing sugar until stiff and place in a piping bag fitted with a star nozzle. Pipe rings of cream on to the cooled meringues. Peel and slice the Chinese gooseberries and arrange on top of the cream. Place slices of ice cream over the gooseberries and serve immediately.

Fruit and Rum Babas

SAVARIN DOUGH
350 g/12 oz plain flour
20 g/¾ oz fresh yeast
250 ml/8 fl oz lukewarm milk
4 eggs
40 g/1½ oz castor sugar
25 g/1 oz vanilla sugar
¼ teaspoon salt
150 g/5 oz butter
SYRUP
150 g/5 oz granulated sugar
250 ml/8 fl oz water
grated rind of 1 lemon
4 tablespoons rum
6 tablespoons white wine
FILLING
250 ml/8 fl oz double cream
1 tablespoon icing sugar
1 teaspoon cocoa powder
350 g/12oz drained canned fruit (pineapple, goose-berries, cherries, kumquats, Chinese gooseberries)
50 g/2 oz flaked almonds

Grease about twenty-four 7·5-cm/3-inch savarin tins with butter and sprinkle with flour.

Sift the flour into a bowl and make a well in the centre. Cream the yeast with a little of the milk, then gradually add the remainder. Pour into the well in the flour, cover and leave in a warm place for 15 minutes, until frothy.

Whisk the eggs with the sugar until frothy, add the vanilla sugar and salt. Melt the butter without allowing it to become hot and add to the egg mixture. Pour into the yeast mixture in the bowl and beat in the rest of the flour to give a loose dough. Cover and leave to stand for a further 10 minutes. Half-fill the savarin tins with the dough mixture, cover and leave to rise for 15 minutes.

Preheat the oven to moder-ately hot (200°C, 400°F, Gas Mark 6) and bake for 30 minutes in the centre of the

oven. Turn the savarins out on to a wire rack and allow to cool.

Dissolve the sugar in the water with the lemon rind, rum and white wine, stirring continuously over a low heat until the sugar has completely dissolved. Bring to the boil and cook for 5–10 minutes. Place the babas upside down on a plate and spoon over the warm syrup; they must be completely soaked.

Whip the cream with the sifted icing sugar until stiff and divide in half. Mix one half with the sifted cocoa powder. Fill a piping bag fitted with a star nozzle with the plain and chocolate cream one after the other, and pipe a rosette of cream into the centre of each baba.

Cut the fruit into small pieces and decorate the babas with the fruit and flaked almonds.

Cook's Tip

If you have only 12 savarin tins you must bake the babas in two lots. Instead of savarin tins you can use ring moulds or make more savarin tins out of aluminium foil.

Desserts with a Difference

Italian Cassata

1 sandwich cake (see below)
FILLING
350 g/12 oz curd cheese
2 tablespoons double cream
60 g/2 oz castor sugar
1 tablespoon orange liqueur
2 tablespoons finely chopped
  glacé fruit
ICING
225 g/8 oz plain chocolate
4–5 tablespoons strong black
  coffee
100 g/4 oz butter
glacé fruit to decorate

Make the sandwich cake
according to the basic recipe
(see page 228), then turn into a
greased 1-kg/2-lb loaf tin.
Bake in a moderate oven
(160°C, 325°F. Gas Mark 3)
for 45 minutes and leave to
cool on a wire rack. Trim the
cake if necessary and cut into
four layers horizontally.

Sieve the cheese and stir
until smooth with the cream,
sugar and orange liqueur. Add
the chopped glacé fruit. Cover
three layers of the cake with
this filling and place one upon
the other. Top with the final
cake layer, pressing the cake
down slightly so that it is
compact in shape. Leave to
stand for 2 hours in the
refrigerator.

Break the chocolate into
small pieces and stir into the
coffee over a moderate heat
until melted. Stir in the butter
in small pieces until a completely smooth creamy mixture
is obtained. Place in the
refrigerator until it begins to
set. Cover the sides and top of
the cake with this chocolate
cream.

Fill a piping bag fitted with
a star nozzle with the remainder of the cream and
decorate the cake with rosettes
and garlands, as illustrated.
Top the rosettes of cream with
glacé fruit cut into small
pieces. Wrap the cake carefully in foil and leave for 1
day in the refrigerator before
serving.

Christmas Stollen

1 kg/2¼ lb plus 200 g/7 oz
  plain flour
100 g/4 oz fresh yeast
450 ml/¾ pint lukewarm milk
100 g/4 oz castor sugar
2 eggs
few drops of vanilla essence
grated rind of 1 lemon
¼ teaspoon salt
400 g/14 oz butter
350 g/12 oz raisins
100 g/4 oz blanched almonds,
  chopped
100 g/4 oz candied lemon peel,
  chopped
50 g/2 oz candied orange peel,
  chopped
1 tablespoon rum
TOPPING
150 g/5 oz butter, melted
150 g/5 oz icing sugar

Line a baking tray with buttered greaseproof paper.

Sift the 1 kg/2¼ lb flour into a large bowl and make a well in the centre. Cream the yeast with a little milk then gradually add the remaining milk. Stir in a little sugar, pour into the well and sprinkle with a little of the flour. Cover and leave in a warm place for 15 minutes, until frothy. Mix the rest of the sugar with the eggs, vanilla, lemon rind and salt, add to the yeast mixture and work in with the rest of the flour to give a dry firm dough. Knead until smooth then cover and leave to rise for 1 hour.

Work the butter and the remaining 200 g/7 oz flour together, knead into the risen dough, cover and leave to stand for a further 15 minutes. Meanwhile, mix the raisins, almonds and chopped peel together, sprinkle with the rum, cover and leave to steep. Then quickly work this fruit mixture into the dough, cover and leave to stand in a warm place for a further 15 minutes.

Divide the dough into three portions and roll each piece into a 30-cm/12-inch length. Roll gently so that the dough is thinner in the middle than at the ends. Fold the dough over lengthways, making a 15-cm/6-inch length – this gives the typical stollen shape – and place on the baking tray. Repeat using the other two pieces of dough. Cover the loaves and leave to stand for a further 20 minutes, until increased in size. Preheat the oven to moderately hot (200°C, 400°F, Gas Mark 6).

Bake the loaves for 25–30 minutes. While still hot, brush with the melted butter and dredge generously with sifted icing sugar.

Almond Stollen

Omit the raisins, almonds, lemon peel, orange peel and rum. Prepare the dough as for the Christmas Stollen, and after the second rising knead in 250 g/9 oz chopped blanched almonds and 250 g/9 oz chopped candied lemon peel. Leave to stand for a further 15 minutes then continue as for Christmas Stollen.

Christmas Baking Begins Early

Traditional Fruit Loaf

75 g/3 oz dried stoned prunes
175 g/6 oz dried pears
75 g/3 oz dried figs
50 g/2 oz raisins
50 g/2 oz currants
50 g/2 oz chopped mixed peel
300 ml/½ pint hot black tea
50 g/2 oz sugar
¼ teaspoon ground cinnamon
pinch each of ground cloves,
    ground aniseed and salt
2 tablespoons rum
2 tablespoons lemon juice
200 g/7 oz plain flour
50 g/2 oz hazelnuts, finely
    chopped
50 g/2 oz walnuts, finely
    chopped
STARTER DOUGH
2 tablespoons milk
4 tablespoons water
1 teaspoon oil
1 teaspoon dried yeast
2 tablespoons lukewarm water

1 teaspoon castor sugar
2 teaspoons salt
50 g/2 oz strong plain flour
50 g/2 oz rye flour
DECORATION
25 g/1 oz blanched almonds,
    halved
glacé cherries
angelica

First make the starter dough.
Combine the milk, 4 tablespoons water and the oil in a
saucepan and bring to the boil.
Allow to cool until lukewarm.
Blend the yeast with 2 tablespoons lukewarm water and the
sugar and leave for 5 minutes.
Add to the milk mixture with
the salt. Stir this liquid into the
plain and rye flours until well
blended. Cover and leave to
stand for 12–18 hours.

Meanwhile chop the prunes,
pears and figs. Place in a bowl
with the raisins, currants and
mixed peel. Pour on the freshly
made tea, cover and leave to
soak overnight. Add the sugar,

spices, salt, rum and lemon
juice to the fruit. Stir all the
ingredients well, cover and
leave to stand for a further
30 minutes.

Grease a 20-cm/8-inch cake
tin with butter or margarine.
Preheat the oven to moderate
(180°C, 350°F, Gas Mark 4).

Add the fruit mixture to the
starter dough with the sifted
flour and chopped nuts. Mix
all thoroughly until well
combined and place in the cake
tin. Decorate with almond
halves, glacé cherries and strips
of angelica, as illustrated. Bake
for 1 hour 10 minutes.

Cook's Tip

This fruit loaf is
especially delicious made
with the given mixture
of various fruits. Should
you not have one kind of
dried fruit, you can in-
crease the quantity of the
other fruits accordingly.
Take care that your fruit
is made up of a mixture
of light and dark fruits.
Fruit loaves keep fresh
and moist for a long time
if stored in an airtight
container or wrapped
tightly in foil.

Christmas Baking Begins Early

Christmas Loaf

400 g/14 oz dried pears
300 g/11 oz dried prunes
400 g/14 oz dried figs
150 g/5 oz walnuts
100 g/3½ oz raisins
125 g/4½ oz sultanas
100 g/4 oz chopped mixed peel
200 g/7 oz castor sugar
2 teaspoons ground cinnamon
1 teaspoon each ground cloves,
* aniseed and salt*
2 tablespoons rum
1 kg/2¼ lb plain flour
40 g/1½ oz fresh yeast
1 teaspoon sugar
RYE BREAD DOUGH
900 g/2 lb rye flour
150 ml/¼ pint hot milk
25 g/1 oz fresh yeast
2 teaspoons castor sugar
1 teaspoon salt
25 g/1 oz butter, melted
1 tablespoon oil

Soak the pears and prunes in
900 ml/1½ pints water, cover
and cook until soft. Drain and
reserve the liquor. Stone the
prunes and coarsely chop with
the pears, figs and walnuts.
Add the raisins, sultanas,
mixed peel, sugar, spices, salt
and rum and cover.
   Gradually whisk 300 ml/
½ pint hot water into 50 g/2 oz
of the rye flour. Cover and
leave for 1½ hours then stir in
the hot milk. Cream the yeast
with the sugar and 150 ml/¼ pint
lukewarm water and leave for 10
minutes. Stir into the flour paste
with the salt, butter and oil.
Work in the remaining rye flour.
Cover and leave until risen.
   Sift the plain flour into a
bowl and form a well. Cream
the yeast with the sugar and
400 ml/14 fl oz of the cooled
fruit liquor; pour into the well.
Sprinkle over a little of the
flour and leave until frothy.
Add the fruit and nut mixture,
work to a dough. Leave for
15 minutes then shape into four
oval loaves.
   Divide the rye bread dough
into four and roll out each
quarter into an oval large
enough to enclose a fruit loaf.
Brush each fruit loaf with
water and wrap in the rye
dough, sealing the edges with
water. Place on greased baking
trays and brush with water.
Leave to stand for 15 minutes.
Preheat the oven to moderately
hot (190°C, 375°F, Gas Mark
5) and bake for 1¼–1½ hours.

Christmas Baking Begins Early

Italian Panettone

400 g/14 oz plain flour
25 g/1 oz fresh yeast
50 g/2 oz castor sugar
150 ml/¼ pint lukewarm milk
100 g/4 oz butter, melted
3 egg yolks
1 teaspoon salt
pinch of grated nutmeg
grated rind of ½ lemon
100 g/4 oz chopped mixed peel
50 g/2 oz raisins
1 egg yolk, beaten to glaze

Line a deep 18-cm/7-inch cake tin with buttered greaseproof paper.

Sift the flour into a bowl and make a well in the centre. Cream the yeast with a little of the sugar and the milk and pour into the well. Sprinkle with a little of the flour and leave in a warm place for 15 minutes, until frothy. Add the remaining sugar, the melted butter, egg yolks, salt, nutmeg and lemon rind and beat in all the flour until the mixture forms a soft dough. Knead the dough for about 10 minutes then cover and leave to rise until doubled in size (about 1 hour). Turn on to a lightly floured board and knead in the chopped peel and raisins. Form the dough into a ball, place in the tin, cover and leave to stand until the dough reaches the top of the tin. Preheat the oven to moderately hot (200°C, 400°F, Gas Mark 6).

Brush the cake with beaten egg yolk, cut a cross on the top and bake for 20 minutes. Reduce the oven temperature to moderate (180°C, 350°F, Gas Mark 4) and continue to bake for a further 45 minutes. Allow the cake to cool slightly in the tin, then turn out on to a wire rack and leave until completely cold. Remove the greaseproof paper just before cutting the cake.

Honey Cakes

500 g/1 lb honey
6 tablespoons water
500 g/1 lb black treacle
700 g/1½ lb wholemeal flour
300 g/10 oz rye flour
1 tablespoon baking powder
1 teaspoon bicarbonate of soda
1 tablespoon milk
FILLING
100 g/4 oz almond paste
130 g/4½ oz castor sugar
1 egg white
1 tablespoon rum
100 g/4 oz candied fruit,
  chopped
100 g/4 oz blanched almonds,
  chopped
milk to brush
ICING
300 g/11 oz plain chocolate
glacé cherries and angelica

Melt the honey and gradually bring to the boil with the water and treacle. Leave to cool. Work in the flours and the baking powder. Dissolve the bicarbonate of soda in the milk and stir into the mixture. Wrap in foil and leave for 2 days at room temperature.

Break the almond paste into small pieces and mix with the sugar, egg white, rum, candied fruit and almonds. Stand over a pan of hot water and mix well.

Preheat the oven to moderately hot (190°C, 375°F, Gas Mark 5). Grease three baking trays. Divide the cake dough into three portions. Roll each piece out to a thickness of 1·5 cm/¾ inch and cut out two heart shapes from each portion. Spread the marzipan filling over the centre of half the hearts, brush the edges with milk, top with a second heart and press the edges well together.

Bake the cakes for 30–35 minutes then leave to cool. Melt the chocolate in a basin over hot water, ice the cakes all over and top with cherries and angelica as illustrated.

111

Gingerbread House

1 kg/2 lb thick honey
250 ml/8 fl oz water
650 g/1¼ lb rye flour
500 g/1 lb plain wholemeal flour
200 g/7 oz chopped mixed peel
1 teaspoon ground ginger
1 teaspoon ground cinnamon
¼ teaspoon grated nutmeg
1 teaspoon bicarbonate of soda
DECORATION
20–30 blanched almonds
2 egg whites
500 g/1 lb icing sugar
1 tablespoon lemon juice
coloured sugar balls

Bring the honey to the boil with the water, stirring continuously, then leave to cool. Place the flours in a large mixing bowl and sprinkle with the mixed peel and spices. Form a well in the centre and pour in the honey which should be almost cold. Knead all the ingredients to obtain a soft dough. Finally mix the bicarbonate of soda into the dough. Place the dough in a polythene bag, seal and leave to stand for 1–2 days; this will make the gingerbread more tasty.

To construct the house it is advisable to cut out a cardboard pattern for the walls and roof, corresponding in size with the illustration. Lightly grease two baking trays. Preheat the oven to moderately hot (200°C, 400°F, Gas Mark 6). Roll part of the honey dough into 18 long sausage shapes, 40 cm/16 inches long and 1·5 cm/¾ inch in diameter.

Place side by side on one of the baking trays, leaving about 3 mm/⅛ inch between each. They should form a rectangle 40 × 25 cm/16 × 10 inches. During baking the gaps close up and form the walls of the log cabin. Bake in the centre of the oven for 20–30 minutes.

Roll out the rest of the dough to 1 cm/½ inch thick. Cut out one piece of about 25 × 15 cm/10 × 6 inches and a second piece 35 × 28 cm/14 × 11 inches. Place these pieces on the baking tray, prick with a fork and bake for 12–18 minutes in the centre of the oven. From the 40 × 25-cm/16 × 10-inch piece which was baked first, cut out with a sharp knife the front, back and side walls of the house, using the cardboard pattern. Cut out a door and window in the front wall. From the flat pieces of dough cut out a base and two roof pieces using the cardboard pattern as a guide. Roll out

the rest of the dough to 5 mm/¼ inch thick, cut out 20 small biscuits and place an almond on each. Also cut out pieces for the chimney and strips for the fence as illustrated and bake for 12–15 minutes.

Lightly whisk the egg whites until frothy, then gradually beat in the sifted icing sugar until a thick icing is obtained. Finally beat in the lemon juice. Assemble the sections of the house, using the icing to hold the pieces together; leave the icing to dry completely at each stage before constructing the next section. Coat the roof and chimney with icing to resemble freshly fallen snow. Decorate the house as you choose or as illustrated with the ginger biscuits, sugar balls and almonds.

Christmas Treats for Children

Gingerbread Family

90 g/3¼ oz margarine
275 g/10 oz clear honey
115 g/4½ oz castor sugar
1½ teaspoons ground ginger
¼ teaspoon ground allspice
¼ teaspoon ground cinnamon
7 g/¼ oz cocoa powder
675 g/1½ lb plain flour
1 teaspoon bicarbonate of soda
pinch of salt
2 eggs
ICING
1 egg white
175–225 g/6–8 oz icing sugar
75 g/3 oz plain chocolate
blanched almonds, pistachio
  nuts, glacé cherries, raisins,
  etc., to decorate

Stir the margarine, honey, sugar, spices and cocoa powder together and warm over a low heat until the sugar is completely dissolved. Leave to cool.

Sift the flour and bicarbonate of soda into a bowl and knead in the salt, eggs and honey mixture to obtain a smooth dough. Cover and leave to stand overnight at room temperature.

Grease two baking trays. Preheat the oven to moderately hot (200°C, 400°F, Gas Mark 6). Roll out the dough to 5 mm/¼ inch thick and cut out figures using a gingerbread cutter. Place on the trays and bake for 12–15 minutes in the centre of the oven. Remove from the baking tray while still warm and cool on a wire rack.

Whisk the egg white stiffly with the sifted icing sugar. Decorate the figures with the piped icing, melted chocolate and the nuts and fruit, as illustrated.

Shortbread Christmas Tree

SHORTBREAD
300 g/11 oz plain flour
100 g/4 oz icing sugar
150 g/5½ oz butter, softened
1 egg
FILLING
250 ml/8 fl oz milk
1 tablespoon sugar
2 tablespoons custard powder
2 egg whites
2 tablespoons icing sugar
DECORATION
4 tablespoons apricot jam
100 g/4 oz desiccated coconut
chocolate and coloured icing,
  hundreds and thousands,
  silver balls and chopped nuts

Cut out from cardboard a Christmas tree pattern 33 cm/13 inches high and 28 cm/11 inches wide at the widest point. Sift the flour and icing sugar into a bowl with the butter and egg, and mix until a dough is formed. Cover and leave for 2 hours in the refrigerator.

Prepare a custard from the milk, sugar and custard powder, following the instructions on the packet. Leave to cool. Whisk the egg whites until stiff then whisk in the sifted icing sugar. Fold into the cooled custard. Preheat the oven to moderately hot (190°C, 375°F, Gas Mark 5).

Roll out the shortbread dough, cut out two trees, and from the trimmings cut several small shapes for decoration. Bake for 15–20 minutes. While still warm cover one tree with the custard filling and place the second tree on top. Leave to cool.

Warm the jam, spread on the tree and sprinkle generously with desiccated coconut. Ice and decorate the small biscuit shapes and attach to the Christmas tree with jam.

Austrian Jam Rings

400 g / 14 oz plain flour
200 g / 7 oz butter, cut into flakes
3 egg yolks
100 g / 4 oz castor sugar
25 g / 1 oz vanilla sugar
grated rind and juice of 1 lemon
50 g / 2 oz ground hazelnuts
100 g / 4 oz strawberry jam
icing sugar to sprinkle

Sift the flour into a mixing bowl and add the butter. Put the egg yolks, sugar, vanilla sugar, lemon rind and hazelnuts in the centre and knead all the ingredients to a pastry dough. Wrap in foil or cling film and leave in the refrigerator for 2 hours.

Preheat the oven to moderately hot (200°C, 400°F, Gas Mark 6). Roll out the pastry on a floured surface to a thickness of about 5 mm/¼ inch, and cut into an equal number of 6-cm/2½-inch circles and rings. Place on a greased baking tray and bake for 10 minutes, until golden brown.

Carefully lift the circles and rings from the baking tray with a palette knife and leave to cool on a wire rack. Mix the jam with the lemon juice. Sift icing sugar generously over the ring biscuits. Spread the round biscuits with the jam and put a ring biscuit on the top of each.

Almond Ring Biscuits

4 hard-boiled egg yolks
200 g / 7 oz butter, softened
80 g / 3 oz icing sugar
few drops of vanilla essence
pinch of salt
300 g / 10½ oz plain flour
120 g / 4 oz almonds
100 g / 3½ oz castor sugar
2 egg yolks
6 tablespoons redcurrant jelly
icing sugar to sprinkle

Press the hard-boiled egg yolks through a sieve and beat with the butter and sifted icing sugar until well mixed. Add the vanilla essence, salt and sifted flour and mix all the ingredients to a firm dough. Wrap in foil or cling film and leave for 2 hours in the refrigerator.

Blanch the almonds in boiling water, peel and chop coarsely, then toss in the sugar.

Preheat the oven to moderately hot (200°C, 400°F, Gas Mark 6). Roll out the dough to 3 mm/⅛ inch thick and with a biscuit ring cutter, cut out rings about 5 cm/2 inches in diameter. Beat the fresh egg yolks, brush one side of the rings and sprinkle with the sugared almond mixture. Place on a baking tray with the almond side uppermost and bake for 10–15 minutes. Remove with a palette knife and cool on a wire rack.

Sandwich the rings together with redcurrant jelly and sprinkle with sifted icing sugar.

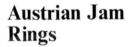

Christmas Baking from Abroad

Swiss Honey Bars

350 g/12 oz thick honey
350 g/12 oz sugar
90 g/3½ oz blanched almonds
90 g/3½ oz hazelnuts
90 g/3½ oz walnuts
250 g/9 oz chopped mixed peel
grated rind of 1 lemon
575 g/1¼ lb plain flour
1 teaspoon ground cinnamon
2 teaspoons ground cloves
generous pinch of grated nutmeg
½ teaspoon bicarbonate of soda
2 tablespoons arrack or ouzo
2 tablespoons cherry brandy

Bring the honey to the boil with 250 g/9 oz of the sugar, stirring continuously. Finely chop the almonds, hazelnuts and walnuts. Combine the nuts with the mixed peel, lemon rind and sifted flour. Stir in the cinnamon, cloves, nutmeg and bicarbonate of soda and

mix well with the hot honey mixture. Knead in the arrack and cherry brandy, form into a ball and leave to stand at room temperature for 1 day.

Preheat the oven to moderate (180°C, 350°F, Gas Mark 4). Grease a baking tray and roll out the dough to 1 cm/½ inch thick. Place on the baking tray and bake for 30–35 minutes in the centre of the oven. Bring the remaining sugar to the boil with a little water. Spread quickly over the cake while still warm and cut into bars on the baking tray. Leave to cool.

Viennese Vanilla Crescents

50 g/2 oz blanched almonds
50 g/2 oz hazelnuts
280 g/10 oz plain flour
70 g/2½ oz castor sugar
pinch of salt
200 g/7 oz butter, cut into flakes
2 egg yolks
75 g/3 oz vanilla sugar
25 g/1 oz icing sugar

Finely grate the almonds and hazelnuts. Place the sifted flour in a mixing bowl with the nuts, sugar, salt, butter and egg yolks, and knead to a soft dough. Wrap in foil or cling film and leave for 2 hours in the refrigerator.

Preheat the oven to moderately hot (190°C, 375°F, Gas Mark 5). Form the dough a little at a time into small rolls

the thickness of a pencil. Cut the rolls into 5-cm/2-inch pieces and curve in crescents. Bake in the centre of the oven for 10 minutes until golden. Mix the vanilla sugar with the sifted icing sugar and toss the biscuits in this while still warm.

Cook's Tip

To store the biscuits, place in layers between greaseproof paper in a tin; this will avoid breakage.

Christmas Baking from Abroad

American Ginger Slices

6 whole preserved gingers
150 g/5¼ oz butter or margarine
100 g/4 oz castor sugar
1 egg
pinch of salt
¼ teaspoon ground ginger
300 g/11 oz plain flour
1 egg yolk to glaze

Very finely chop 3 of the whole gingers and dice the remainder. Cream the butter or margarine with the sugar, egg, salt, ground ginger and finely chopped ginger. Sift in the flour and work quickly together to obtain a smooth dough. Form into a ball, wrap in foil or cling film and leave for 2 hours in the refrigerator.

Preheat the oven to moderately hot (200°C, 400°F, Gas Mark 6). Divide the dough into three and roll out one piece at a time on a floured board to about 5 mm/¼ inch thick. Cut out oblongs about 6 × 3·5 cm/2½ × 1½ inches. Place on a baking tray. Beat the egg yolk with a little water. Brush the biscuits with egg yolk, sprinkle with the diced ginger and bake in the centre of the oven for 15 minutes. Remove from the baking tray with a palette knife and leave to cool on a wire rack.

Danish Cookies

250 g/8 oz butter or margarine
200 g/7 oz sugar
125 g/4 oz golden syrup
75 g/2½ oz blanched almonds, chopped
75 g/2½ oz candied lemon peel, chopped
½ teaspoon ground cloves
2 teaspoons ground cinnamon
½ teaspoon ground ginger
¼ teaspoon bicarbonate of soda
500 g/1 lb plain flour

Melt the butter or margarine with the sugar and syrup. Remove from the heat and stir in the almonds, chopped peel, cloves, cinnamon and ginger.

Dissolve the bicarbonate of soda in a little boiling water, stir into the syrup mixture and leave to cool. Sift and knead in the flour. Form the dough into two rolls, wrap in foil or cling film and leave for 24 hours in the refrigerator.

Grease two baking trays. Preheat the oven to moderately hot (200°C, 400°F, Gas Mark 6). Cut the rolls of dough into slices 5 mm/¼ inch thick. Place on the baking trays, allowing room for spreading, and bake for 8–10 minutes. Remove from the baking trays with a palette knife and leave to cool on a wire rack.

Christmas Cakes and Biscuits

Aniseed Biscuits

4 eggs, separated
225 g/8 oz icing sugar
pinch of salt
300 g/11 oz plain flour
2 teaspoons ground aniseed

Grease a baking tray and
sprinkle with flour.
Cream the egg yolks with the
sifted icing sugar and salt
until pale and light. Whisk the
egg whites until very stiff, then
fold into the yolk mixture. Sift
the flour and aniseed on to
this mixture and fold in quickly
but thoroughly. Fill a piping
bag fitted with a plain nozzle
with the biscuit mixture and
pipe in small rounds on to the
baking tray. Leave to dry out
overnight.
  Preheat the oven to
moderate (160°C, 325°F, Gas
Mark 3), and bake towards the
top of the oven for 20 minutes.
Cool on a wire rack.

Cook's Tip
To make Cinnamon
Biscuits, substitute 2
teaspoons ground cinna-
mon for the ground
aniseed.

Chocolate Macaroons

100 g/4 oz plain chocolate
4 egg whites
200 g/7 oz castor sugar
225 g/8 oz ground almonds

Line a baking tray with non-
stick baking parchment or rice
paper. Preheat the oven to
moderate (180°C, 350°F, Gas
Mark 4).
  Grate the chocolate. Whisk
the egg whites until stiff. Add
the sugar gradually and
continue whisking until the
mixture is thick and glossy.
Fold in the ground almonds
and grated chocolate. Drop
spoonfuls of the mixture on to
the baking tray, leaving space
between each biscuit. Bake for
15–20 minutes. Do not let the
macaroons become too dark or
they will taste bitter.
  Cool on the baking tray,
then carefully peel the
macaroons off the non-stick
paper or cut around each
biscuit on the edible rice
paper.

125

Nutmeg Biscuits

125 g/4 oz butter
125 g/4 oz castor sugar
1 egg
grated rind of ½ lemon
generous pinch of grated nutmeg
pinch each of ground cinnamon and ground cloves
125 g/4 oz plain flour
125 g/4 oz hazelnuts, finely chopped
125 g/4 oz fresh white breadcrumbs
1 egg yolk, beaten to glaze
50 g/2 oz blanched almonds

Beat the butter with the sugar, egg, lemon rind and spices. Mix the sifted flour with the hazelnuts and breadcrumbs, add to the butter mixture and knead all the ingredients quickly to a dough. Cover and leave for 2 hours in the refrigerator.

Preheat the oven to moderately hot (200°C, 400°F, Gas Mark 6). Roll out the dough to 5 mm/¼ inch thick. Cut out small scalloped arcs 6 cm/2½ inches long and 2·5 cm/1 inch wide. Place on greased baking trays and brush with beaten egg yolk. Place a blanched almond on each biscuit and bake for 10–15 minutes.

Cook's Tip
If you do not have the proper biscuit cutter, make a cardboard pattern and use it to help you cut out the arcs.

Iced Lemon Bars

150 g/5 oz butter
125 g/4 oz castor sugar
1 egg
generous pinch each of ground cinnamon, ground cloves and grated nutmeg
grated rind of 1 lemon
125 g/4 oz plain flour
125 g/4 oz ground almonds
125 g/4 oz fresh white breadcrumbs
ICING
200 g/7 oz icing sugar
2–3 tablespoons lemon juice
30 g/1 oz candied lemon peel
30 g/1 oz candied orange peel

Beat the butter with the sugar until pale and creamy. Stir in the egg, spices and lemon rind. Sift in the flour, gradually add the almonds and breadcrumbs and knead to a smooth soft dough. Wrap in foil or cling film and leave for 2 hours in the refrigerator.

Preheat the oven to moderately hot (200°C, 400°F, Gas Mark 6). Roll out the dough on a floured board to 5 mm/¼ inch thick and cut out bars 2·5 × 6 cm/1 × 2½ inches. Place on greased baking trays, allowing room between each for spreading. Bake for 10–15 minutes then remove with a palette knife and place on a wire rack.

Sift the icing sugar and stir in the lemon juice until smooth. Use to thickly ice the biscuits when they are slightly cooled. Cut the lemon and orange peel into thin strips and place on the icing while still soft.

Christmas Cakes and Biscuits

Chocolate Orange Cookies

100 g/4 oz plain chocolate
125 g/4½ oz butter or margarine
125 g/4½ oz castor sugar
pinch of salt
1 egg
grated rind of 1 orange
200 g/7 oz plain flour
1 teaspoon baking powder
ICING
100 g/4 oz icing sugar
1–2 tablespoons orange juice

Coarsely grate the chocolate. Beat the butter or margarine with the sugar, salt, egg and orange rind. Sift in the flour with the baking powder, add the grated chocolate and quickly knead all the ingredients to a workable dough. Form into a ball, wrap in foil or cling film and leave for 2 hours in the refrigerator.

Preheat the oven to moderately hot (200°C, 400°F, Gas Mark 6). Roll out the dough on a floured board to 5 mm/¼ inch thick and cut out rounds 5 cm/2 inches in diameter. Place on greased baking trays, allowing room for spreading, and bake for 10–15 minutes. Carefully remove from the baking trays with a palette knife and leave to cool on a wire rack.

Sift the icing sugar and stir in the orange juice until smooth. Spread this icing over the top of the cookies and leave to set.

Crumbly Almond Hearts

250 g/9 oz butter
120 g/4½ oz icing sugar
2 egg yolks
100 g/4 oz ground almonds
350 g/12 oz plain flour
40 blanched almonds, halved

Beat the butter with the sifted icing sugar and 1 egg yolk until pale and creamy. Add the ground almonds and sifted flour and knead quickly to a firm dough. Form into a ball, wrap in foil or cling film and leave for 2 hours in the refrigerator.

Preheat the oven to moderately hot (200°C, 400°F, Gas Mark 6). Roll out the dough on a floured board to 5 mm/¼ inch thick and cut out 40 small heart shapes. Place on a large baking tray, beat the second egg yolk, brush the

biscuits with this and place two almond halves on each. Bake for 10–12 minutes.

Allow the biscuits to cool slightly on the baking tray, then remove to a wire rack and leave until completely cool.

Christmas Night Gâteau

SPONGE MIXTURE
4 eggs, separated
3 tablespoons water
180 g/6 oz castor sugar
1 tablespoon vanilla sugar
150 g/5¼ oz plain flour
100 g/3¼ oz cornflour
2 teaspoons baking powder
FILLING AND TOPPING
7 g/¼ oz powdered gelatine
600 ml/1 pint double cream
150 g/5 oz castor sugar
40 g/1½ oz cocoa powder
1 tablespoon boiling water
1 tablespoon rum
3 tablespoons cranberry jelly
DECORATION
100 g/4 oz plain chocolate
8 glacé cherries
1 teaspoon icing sugar
25 g/1 oz toasted flaked
  almonds

Grease the base of a 23-cm/9-inch cake tin with butter or margarine. Preheat the oven to moderately hot (190°C, 375°F, Gas Mark 5).

Beat the egg yolks with the water, half the sugar and the vanilla sugar until pale and creamy. Whisk the egg whites until stiff and fold in the remaining sugar, then carefully fold into the egg yolk mixture. Sift the flour with the cornflour and baking powder and carefully fold into the mixture. Turn into the prepared tin, smooth the surface and bake for 30–40 minutes. Cool on a wire rack. Leave the cake to stand overnight if possible then cut through twice to make three layers.

Dissolve the gelatine in 2 tablespoons water over a gentle heat. Whip the cream with the sugar until stiff. Cream the cocoa powder with the boiling water and rum, cool and mix a quarter of the cream with it. Spread this chocolate cream thickly on the first layer of cake and place the second layer on top. Warm the cranberry jelly, cool slightly and mix with the dissolved gelatine into a second quarter of the cream. Cover the second cake layer with this mixture and top with the last cake layer. Cover the cake all over with some of the remaining cream, place the rest in a piping bag fitted with a star nozzle and pipe 16 rosettes around the top of the cake.

Melt half the chocolate by standing in a basin over a pan of hot water and spread thinly on to greaseproof paper or foil. When the chocolate has set, dip a small star-shaped cutter into hot water and cut out 16 star shapes. Place a chocolate star and halved glacé cherry on each rosette. Coarsely grate the remaining chocolate. Sprinkle over the centre of the cake, sift lightly with icing sugar and decorate the sides of the cake with flaked almonds.

Cook's Tip

From the block of chocolate you can also make chocolate caraque, as illustrated. Spread the melted chocolate on to a clean flat surface. When the chocolate has just set, scrape off shavings with the blade of a knife. Leave the shavings to set hard then sprinkle on to the cake.

Christmas Specialities

Chocolate Log

SPONGE MIXTURE
*4 eggs, separated, plus 2 egg
    yolks
80 g/3 oz castor sugar
grated rind of ¼ lemon
80 g/3 oz plain flour*
FILLING AND TOPPING
*350 g/12 oz plain chocolate
225 g/8 oz butter
125 g/4½ oz icing sugar
1 tablespoon rum
3 glacé cherries
1 teaspoon chopped pistachio
    nuts*

Line a 33 × 23-cm/13 × 9-inch
Swiss roll tin with greased
greaseproof paper. Preheat the
oven to hot (220°C, 425°F,
Gas Mark 7).
    Beat all the egg yolks with 1
tablespoon sugar and the lemon
rind until pale and creamy.
Whisk the egg whites until
stiff, fold in the remaining
sugar then fold into the egg
yolks. Carefully fold in the
sifted flour. Spread this
mixture evenly over the Swiss
roll tin and bake near the top
of the oven for 10–12 minutes.
    Turn the cake out on to a
clean tea towel sprinkled with
sugar, remove the greaseproof
lining paper and trim off the
edges of the sponge. Cover
with a clean piece of greaseproof
paper and carefully roll up the
cake with the help of the tea
towel, keeping the clean
greaseproof inside. Cool.
    Melt the chocolate in a
basin over hot water. Spread
approximately a quarter of the
chocolate thinly over greaseproof paper and leave to set.
Allow the melted chocolate to
cool. Beat the butter with the
sifted icing sugar until pale
and creamy; keep 2 table-
spoons to one side. Beat the
cooled melted chocolate and
rum into the rest of this butter
cream. Carefully unroll the
cooled cake and spread two-
thirds of the chocolate cream
over it. Roll up again and pipe
the rest of the cream in stripes
along the length of the cake.
    From the thin sheet of
chocolate cut out small leaves,
using a warmed knife. Decorate
the log with the reserved butter
cream, the halved glacé
cherries, chocolate leaves and
pistachio nuts, as illustrated.
Cut off one slice and place
beside the cake.

Fairy Tale Fir Cone Cake

2 (18-cm/7-inch) sandwich
  cakes (see method)
25 g/1 oz cornflour
2 egg yolks
300 ml/½ pint milk
100 g/4 oz castor sugar
250 g/9 oz butter
50 g/2 oz plain chocolate
50 g/2 oz cocoa powder
3 small packets chocolate
  buttons

Make a sandwich cake follow-ing the basic recipe on page 228. Bake in two 18-cm/7-inch greased sandwich tins in a moderately hot oven (190°C, 375°F, Gas Mark 5) for 25 minutes. Cut the cooled cakes into the oval shape of a large fir cone.

Blend the cornflour with the egg yolks and a little of the milk. Dissolve the sugar in the remaining milk and bring to the boil. Pour on to the cornflour mixture, stirring continuously. Return to the heat and bring to the boil, stirring until thickened, then leave to cool. Beat the butter until pale and creamy then gradually stir in the cooled cornflour custard, beating well with each addition. Melt the chocolate in a basin over hot water and mix into the butter cream with the sifted cocoa powder.

Cut horizontally through each cake once to give four layers in all. Sandwich the cakes together with the choco-late butter cream and spread it over the top and sides. Press chocolate buttons over the surface of the cake, slightly overlapping, to cover it completely.

Brussels Fruit Cake

200 g/7 oz crystallised pineapple
200 g/7 oz crystallised pears
90 g/3 oz candied lemon peel
250 g/9 oz red and green glacé
  cherries, halved
225 g/8 oz walnuts, finely
  chopped
110 g/4 oz pecan nuts, finely
  chopped
110 g/4 oz almonds, finely
  chopped
110 g/4 oz hazelnuts, finely
  chopped
400 g/14 oz raisins
5 tablespoons sherry
225 g/8 oz butter
450 g/1 lb castor sugar
pinch each of salt and grated
  nutmeg
6 eggs
450 g/1 lb self-raising flour
sherry to moisten
crystallised and glacé fruit
  to decorate

Finely dice the pineapple, pears and candied peel and mix with the cherries, nuts, raisins and sherry. Leave to stand overnight.

Line two 1-kg/2-lb loaf tins with buttered greaseproof paper. Preheat the oven to moderate (160°C, 325°F, Gas Mark 3).

Beat the butter with the sugar, salt and nutmeg until pale and creamy, then beat in the eggs one at a time. Fold in the sifted flour and finally stir in the fruit and nut mixture. Turn into the prepared tins and bake for 2–2¼ hours.

Remove the cakes from the tins when cool and strip off the greaseproof paper. Wrap each cake in a muslin cloth moistened in sherry, then wrap in foil and leave in the refrigerator for 4 weeks. Every week moisten the muslin with sherry again. Finally decorate the cakes with crystallised and glacé fruit.

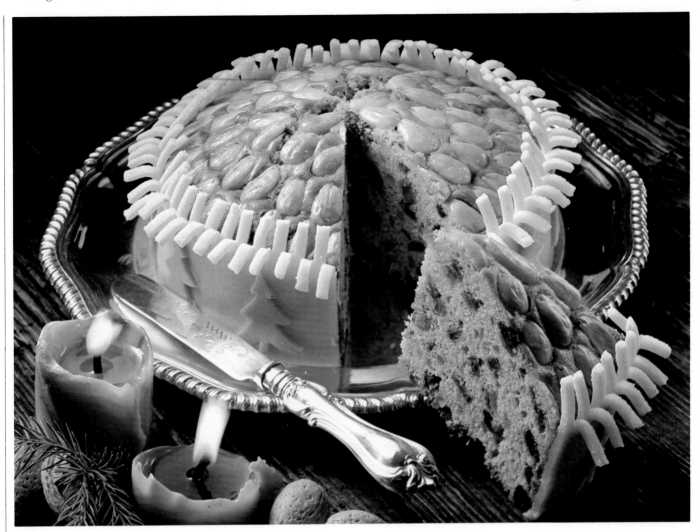

Festive Light Christmas Cake

250 g/9 oz butter
250 g/9 oz castor sugar
¼ teaspoon vanilla essence
generous pinch of salt
1 tablespoon rum
6 eggs
350 g/12 oz plain flour
1 teaspoon baking powder
400 g/14 oz sultanas
50 g/2 oz ground almonds
100 g/4 oz candied lemon peel,
  chopped
100 g/4 oz blanched almonds,
  halved
GLAZE AND DECORATION
2 tablespoons granulated sugar
4 tablespoons water
225 g/8 oz almond paste
2 tablespoons apricot jam
food colourings

Line a 23-cm/9-inch round cake tin with greased greaseproof paper. Preheat the oven to cool (150°C, 300°F, Gas Mark 2).

Beat the softened butter with the castor sugar, vanilla essence, salt and rum until pale and creamy. Stir in the eggs one at a time. If the eggs should curdle the mixture slightly, add a tablespoon of flour. Sift the remaining flour with the baking powder and mix with the sultanas, ground almonds and chopped peel. Fold this flour mixture gradually into the creamed mixture. Turn into the prepared tin, smooth the surface with the back of a wet spoon and arrange the almond halves in a circular pattern on top. Bake the cake for 3–3½ hours. Before removing from the oven test with a skewer; if the skewer comes out clean from the centre, then the cake is cooked through. Allow to stand in the tin for about 15 minutes then place on a wire cooling rack, leaving the greaseproof paper on the cake.

Heat the sugar and water, stirring continuously until the sugar is completely dissolved. Boil for 2–3 minutes. Cover the top of the cake with this glaze and leave to cool.

Spread the sides of the cake with the warmed jam. Roll out the almond paste thinly. Cut pieces to cover the sides of the cake, cutting into strips at the top, as illustrated. Colour the rest of the marzipan with the food colouring of your choice, cut out small Christmas tree shapes and attach to the cake with unbeaten egg white.

Cook's Tip

If you tie a double thickness of brown paper around the outside of the cake tin before baking, this will prevent the edges of the cake becoming brown and overcooked before the inside is cooked through.
The undecorated cake will keep well if wrapped in greaseproof paper and stored in an airtight tin.

Date and Almond Stollen

500 g/1 lb plain flour
30 g/1 oz fresh yeast
250 ml/8 fl oz lukewarm milk
60 g/2 oz castor sugar
2 eggs
·150 g/5 oz butter, cut into flakes
50 g/2 oz blanched almonds,
   chopped
grated rind of 1 lemon
pinch of salt
FILLING
25 g/1 oz cornflour
450 ml/¾ pint milk
1 egg yolk
100 g/3½ oz castor sugar
250 g/8 oz dates, finely chopped
15 g/½ oz butter
ICING
200 g/7 oz icing sugar
1 egg white
juice of 1 lemon
2 tablespoons toasted flaked
   almonds

Grease a baking tray with butter or margarine.

Sift the flour into a bowl and form a well in the centre. Cream the yeast with a little of the milk and 1 tablespoon of the sugar. Add the remaining milk and pour into the flour. Sprinkle a little flour over it, cover and leave to stand for 15 minutes in a warm place, until frothy.

Beat the eggs and mix with the remaining sugar, the butter, almonds, lemon rind and salt. Add to the flour and yeast mixture and knead all the ingredients well for 5–10 minutes, to form a smooth elastic dough. Cover and leave to rise for 30 minutes.

Blend the cornflour with a little of the milk, the egg yolk and sugar. Bring the dates to the boil in the remaining milk. Stir the milk and dates into the cornflour mixture then add the butter. Return to the heat and bring to the boil, stirring

continuously until thickened. Leave the mixture to cool, stirring occasionally to prevent a skin forming.

Lightly knead the dough and roll out to 1 cm/½ inch thick on a floured board. Spread the date mixture evenly over it. Turn both side edges over twice towards the centre and press·together. Place on the baking tray and leave to stand for a further 20 minutes.

Preheat the oven to moderately hot (200°C, 400°F, Gas Mark 6) and bake the stollen for 1 hour. Sift the icing sugar and beat into the egg white with the lemon juice. Ice the stollen while still warm and sprinkle flaked almonds on to the icing before it sets.

Cook's Tip

This stollen tastes best when eaten fresh. However, if well wrapped in foil, it will keep for 3–4 days.

Christmas Specialities

Apricot Plait

500 g / 1 lb plain flour
30 g / 1 oz fresh yeast
250 ml / 8 fl oz lukewarm milk
60 g / 2 oz castor sugar
150 g / 5 oz dried apricots, finely
 chopped
100 g / 3¼ oz blanched almonds,
 chopped
50 g / 2 oz candied lemon peel,
 chopped
25 g / 1 oz candied orange peel,
 chopped
1 tablespoon arrack or ouzo
2 eggs, beaten
150 g / 5 oz butter, cut into flakes
grated rind of 1 lemon
pinch of salt
TOPPING
50 g / 2 oz butter
icing sugar to sprinkle

Grease a narrow 1-kg/2-lb
loaf tin and sprinkle with flour.
 Sift the flour into a bowl and
form a well in the centre.
Cream the yeast with a little

of the milk and 1 teaspoon of
the sugar. Stir in the remaining
milk and pour into the flour.
Sprinkle a little of the flour
over the liquid and leave for
15 minutes, until frothy.
 Mix the apricots with the
almonds, chopped peel and
arrack. To the flour and yeast
mixture add the eggs, remaining
sugar, the butter, lemon rind and
salt, and knead together until
smooth and elastic. Knead in
the fruit mixture, cover and
leave to rise in a warm place
for 30 minutes.
 Divide the dough into three
and form into long rolls.
Weave into a plait, place in the
loaf tin, cover and leave to
stand in a warm place for a
further 20 minutes. Preheat
the oven to moderately hot
(190°C, 375°F, Gas Mark 5).
 Bake for 30–40 minutes.
While still warm brush with
the melted butter and sift
icing sugar generously over the
top and sides.

Soft Fruit Loaf

500 g / 1 lb cottage cheese
500 g / 1 lb plain flour
2 teaspoons baking powder
2 eggs
150 g / 5 oz castor sugar
1 tablespoon vanilla sugar
pinch of salt
1 tablespoon grated lemon rind
1 tablespoon chopped almonds
1 tablespoon raisins
2 tablespoons chopped mixed
 candied fruit
2 tablespoons chopped mixed
 peel
TOPPING
15 g / ¼ oz butter, melted
1 tablespoon icing sugar
1 tablespoon vanilla sugar

Grease a baking tray with
butter or margarine and
sprinkle with flour. Preheat the
oven to moderately hot (190°C,
375°F, Gas Mark 5).
 Press the cottage cheese
through a sieve or liquidise.

Sift the flour with the baking
powder on to a pastry board
and form a well in the centre.
Add the cottage cheese, eggs,
sugar, vanilla sugar, salt,
lemon rind, nuts, fruit and
peel. Mix to a firm dough,
knead lightly and form into a
loaf. Place on a baking tray
and bake for 50–60 minutes.
 Transfer the loaf to a wire
cooling rack and brush with
melted butter while still hot.
Mix the icing sugar and vanilla
sugar and sift generously over
the loaf.

133

Christmas Sweets and Candies

Rich Chocolate Fudge

50 g/2 oz butter
2 egg yolks
100 g/4 oz icing sugar
grated rind of ½ orange
350 g/12 oz plain chocolate
*6 tablespoons strong black tea,
    cooled*
*50 g/2 oz drinking chocolate
    powder*

Line an 18-cm/7-inch shallow
square tin with foil or greaseproof paper. Beat the butter
with the egg yolks and sifted
icing sugar until pale and
creamy. Stir in the grated
orange rind. Coarsely chop the
chocolate and melt in a basin
over a pan of hot water. Stir
the cooled tea and melted
chocolate into the butter
mixture and pour into the
prepared tin. Place in the
refrigerator to set.

When firm cut into 2·5-cm/
1-inch squares and dip in the
sifted chocolate powder.

Cook's Tip

This fudge is delicious
flavoured with 2 tea-
spoons rum in place of
the grated orange rind.
Add the rum to the
melted chocolate then
continue as above.

Quince Diamonds

1·75 kg/4 lb fresh quinces
300 ml/½ pint water
grated rind of 1 orange
grated rind of 1 lemon
1 teaspoon ground cinnamon
1 tablespoon cherry brandy
about 1 kg/2 lb granulated sugar
100 g/4 oz chopped mixed peel

Rub the quinces well with a
damp cloth, quarter, remove
their stalks and the cores. Place
in a pan with the water and
cook over a gentle heat for
45 minutes. Press through a
sieve and weigh the sieved
pulp. Add the orange and
lemon rind, cinnamon and
cherry brandy. Cover and leave
to stand overnight.
    Add 300 g/10 oz sugar for
every 500 g/1 lb of pulp, mix
well and heat until the sugar
dissolves, then reduce to a
thick consistency when the
pulp should come away from

the sides of the pan. Stir
occasionally during cooking.
    Line two 18 × 28-cm/
7 × 11-inch Swiss roll tins
with greaseproof paper and
grease well. Mix the chopped
peel into the quince pulp and
divide the mixture between the
two tins, smoothing over.
Leave to dry out for 3–4
hours in a very cool oven
(110°C, 225°F, Gas Mark ¼)
with the door slightly open.
Leave to cool completely then
cut into diamond shapes and
coat in the remaining sugar.

New Year's Eve Specials

Cinnamon Balls

80 g/3 oz butter or margarine
80 g/3 oz castor sugar
grated rind of ½ lemon
pinch of salt
4 eggs
400 g/14 oz plain flour
1 teaspoon baking powder
100 g/4 oz sugar to sprinkle
2 teaspoons ground cinnamon
oil or fat to deep fry

Beat the butter or margarine with the sugar until light and creamy. Beat in the lemon rind and salt, and the eggs, one at a time. Sift the flour with the baking powder and fold into the mixture with a metal spoon.

Heat the oil or fat to 182°C/360°F in a deep-frying pan. Using two floured teaspoons form the dough into small balls and fry about eight balls at a time in the hot oil until golden. This will take about

5–6 minutes; turn halfway through cooking.

Remove with a draining spoon and drain on absorbent paper. Mix the sugar with the cinnamon and sprinkle over the balls while still warm.

Dutch Raisin Doughnuts

500 g/1 lb plain flour
40 g/1½ oz fresh yeast
100 g/3½ oz castor sugar
6 tablespoons lukewarm milk
pinch of salt
grated rind of 1 lemon
grated rind of 1 orange
2 eggs
75 g/3 oz butter, cut into flakes
100 g/3½ oz raisins
50 g/2 oz currants
75 g/3 oz candied orange peel,
  finely chopped
oil or fat to deep fry

Sift the flour into a bowl and make a well in the centre. Cream the yeast with a little of the sugar and half the milk and pour into the well. Sprinkle with a little of the flour, cover and leave to stand in a warm place for 15 minutes.

Mix the rest of the sugar

with the remaining milk, the salt, lemon and orange rinds, eggs and flaked butter, and beat into the flour. Mix all the ingredients to a stiff dough. Knead for a few minutes then leave to stand in a warm place for 15 minutes. Simmer the raisins and currants for 2 minutes in hot water, drain and mix into the dough with the candied orange peel. Leave the dough to stand for a further 30 minutes.

Heat the oil for frying to 160°C/320°F. Using two floured tablespoons, cut the dough into small doughnuts and fry six at a time in the oil for about 10 minutes, until golden brown. Halfway through the frying time turn the doughnuts with a draining spoon.

Lift out the cooked doughnuts with the draining spoon and drain on absorbent paper.

143

Easter Bread

BASIC YEAST DOUGH
1 kg/2¼ lb plain flour
50 g/2 oz fresh yeast
550 ml/18 fl oz lukewarm milk
200 g/7 oz butter, melted
100 g/3½ oz castor sugar
2 eggs
pinch of salt
grated rind of 1 lemon
FRUIT LOAF
100 g/4 oz blanched almonds,
  chopped
200 g/7 oz candied lemon peel,
  chopped
300 g/11 oz sultanas
1 tablespoon rum
50 g/2 oz butter, melted
50 g/2 oz sugar
PLAITED WREATH
1 egg yolk, beaten to glaze
50 g/2 oz nibbed almonds
50 g/2 oz sugar
2 tablespoons rum

Sift the flour into a bowl and
make a well in the centre.
Cream the yeast with a little of
the milk then stir in the
remaining milk. Pour into the
flour, sprinkle with a little of the
flour and leave to stand in a
warm place for 15 minutes,
until frothy. Pour the melted
butter into the yeast liquid and
mix with the flour, sugar, eggs,
salt and lemon rind, to form a
dough. Knead for 5–10 minutes
until the dough is smooth and
elastic. Cover and leave to rise
for 1 hour in a warm place.
  Mix the almonds, candied
peel, sultanas and rum together
and leave to stand for 30
minutes.
  Divide the dough in two and
knead each half lightly. Mix
one half with the fruit mixture
and leave for 15 minutes. Preheat the oven to moderately hot
(190°C, 375°F, Gas Mark 5).
  Form the fruit dough into a
loaf, place on a greased baking
tray and leave to stand in a
warm place for a further 30
minutes. Cut a cross on the
top of the loaf and bake for
30–40 minutes. While still hot,
brush the loaf with the melted
butter and sprinkle with sugar.
  Divide the remaining dough
into three equal pieces and
form into long strips. Plait
these together, form into a
wreath and brush with beaten
egg yolk. Mix the almonds,
sugar and rum and spread
over the wreath. Bake as for
the fruit loaf.

Bremer Fruit Loaf

750 g/1¼ lb plain flour
45 g/1¼ oz fresh yeast
250 ml/8 fl oz lukewarm milk
100 g/4 oz castor sugar
400 g/12 oz butter
1 tablespoon vanilla sugar
1 teaspoon each salt and ground cardamom
150 g/5 oz blanched almonds, chopped
125 g/4 oz candied lemon peel, chopped
grated rind and juice of 1 lemon
500 g/1 lb raisins

You can bake the Bremer Fruit Loaf either in a loaf tin or on a baking tray. The following recipe uses both ways. Grease a long 1-kg/2-lb loaf tin and a baking tray.

Sift the flour into a bowl and make a well in the centre. Cream the yeast with a little of the milk then add the sugar and the remaining milk. Pour into the flour, cover and leave in a warm place for 15 minutes, until frothy.

Melt the butter, cool slightly and beat with the vanilla sugar, salt and cardamom. Beat the butter mixture into the yeast liquid and flour to obtain a dough. Knead in the almonds, chopped peel, lemon rind and juice and the raisins, until the dough is smooth. Cover and leave to stand in a warm place for a further 40 minutes.

Lightly knead the dough and then halve it. Place one half in the greased loaf tin and leave to stand in a warm place for

30 minutes. Preheat the oven to moderately hot (190°C, 375°F, Gas Mark 5). When the loaf is well risen, place in the oven and bake for 45–50 minutes. Before removing from the oven, test with a skewer. Turn out on a wire rack and leave to cool.

Shape the second half of the dough into a long loaf, place on the greased baking tray and leave to stand in a warm place for 30 minutes. Bake for 45–50 minutes then cool on a wire rack.

Cook's Tip

You can also bake fruit rolls from this dough. When the dough is ready, weigh portions of 40–50 g/1½–2 oz and roll into balls. Place on a greased baking tray, flatten slightly, cover and leave to stand in a warm place for 15 minutes. Before baking brush with beaten egg yolk. Sprinkle with sugar and bake for 20–30 minutes in a moderately hot oven (190°C, 375°F, Gas Mark 5).

Russian Mazurka

5 eggs, separated
175 g / 6 oz castor sugar
2 small lemons
250 g / 9 oz hazelnuts, toasted
  and ground to a powder
TOPPING
250 ml / 8 fl oz double cream
2 tablespoons icing sugar
2 tablespoons rum
coloured sugar Easter eggs

Grease a 20-cm/8-inch cake
tin with butter or margarine.
Preheat the oven to moderate
(180°C, 350°F, Gas Mark 4).
  Beat the egg yolks with the
sugar until pale and creamy.
Grate the rind of both lemons
and squeeze the juice of one.
Add to the egg yolk mixture
and gradually fold in the
hazelnuts. Whisk the egg
whites until stiff and fold
in carefully with a metal spoon.
Place the mixture in the cake
tin, smooth the surface and

bake for 40 minutes. As
soon as the sides of the cake
begin to come away from the
tin, turn off the oven and
leave the cake to stand for
15 minutes in the warm oven.
Turn out to cool on a wire
rack.
  Whip the cream with the
sifted icing sugar and rum.
When stiff enough to stand in
peaks, spread thickly over the
top of the cake and decorate
with Easter eggs.

Country Rice Flan

PASTRY
300 g / 10 oz plain flour
200 g / 7 oz butter, cut into flakes
100 g / 3½ oz castor sugar
1 egg
FILLING
50 g / 2 oz short-grain rice
900 ml / 1½ pints milk
175 g / 6 oz sugar
25 g / 1 oz butter
4 eggs
100 g / 4 oz cream cheese
75 g / 3 oz candied lemon peel,
  chopped
¼ teaspoon ground cinnamon
grated rind of 1 lemon
grated rind of 1 large orange
icing sugar mixed with ground
  cinnamon to sprinkle

Sift the flour into a bowl and
mix in the butter, sugar and
egg to form a dough. Chill in
the refrigerator for 2 hours.

Wash and drain the rice.
Bring the milk to the boil with
the sugar and butter, stir in
the rice and simmer gently,
stirring occasionally, for 1
hour, until thick and creamy.
Remove from the heat. Beat
the eggs with the cream cheese,
chopped peel, cinnamon and
fruit rinds. Gradually stir in
the rice and cool. Preheat the
oven to moderately hot
(200°C, 400°F, Gas Mark 6).
  Roll out two-thirds of the
pastry to line a 20-cm/8-inch
sandwich tin. Prick the base
all over with a fork then fill
with the cooled rice mixture.
Roll out the rest of the pastry,
cut into strips with a pastry
wheel and place on top of the
tart in a lattice pattern. Bake
for 50 minutes, covering with
foil if the top gets too brown.
  Leave in the tin until the
rice is set. Turn out and invert
to serve the lattice on top. Sift
over the sugar and cinnamon.

Gâteau Madame Pompadour

SPONGE MIXTURE
4 eggs, separated, plus 2 egg
  yolks
1 tablespoon hot water
120 g/4 oz castor sugar
150 g/5 oz ground almonds
50 g/2 oz plain flour
pinch of salt
FILLING AND TOPPING
25 g/1 oz cornflour
300 ml/½ pint milk
100 g/4 oz castor sugar
1 tablespoon vanilla sugar
¼ teaspoon vanilla essence
250 g/9 oz butter
50 g/2 oz toasted flaked
  almonds

Grease a 23-cm/9-inch cake
tin and sprinkle with flour.
Preheat the oven to moderate
(180°C, 350°F, Gas Mark 4).

Beat all the egg yolks with
the water and 90 g/3 oz sugar
until pale and creamy. Fold in
the ground almonds and sifted
flour. Whisk the egg whites
with the salt until stiff and fold
in the remaining sugar. Fold
the egg whites into the egg
yolk mixture. Turn into the
prepared tin and bake for 40
minutes, then cool on a wire
rack. Leave to stand for 2 hours
then cut into three layers.

Blend the cornflour with a
little of the milk, the sugar,
vanilla sugar and vanilla
essence. Heat the remaining
milk and pour over the blended
cornflour. Return to the boil,
stirring continuously until
thickened, then cool. Beat the
butter until creamy then gradually beat in the cooled sauce.

Use half this butter cream to
cover two layers of cake and
place the layers one upon the
other. Cover the top and sides
of the cake with the rest of the
cream and sprinkle with
almond flakes. Leave to stand
in a cool place before serving.

Kaiser Franz-Joseph's Cake

100 g/4 oz butter
250 g/9 oz castor sugar
4 eggs, separated, plus 2 egg
  yolks
pinch of salt
1 teaspoon ground cinnamon
1 tablespoon Maraschino
50 g/2 oz fresh white
  breadcrumbs
250 g/9 oz ground almonds
50 g/2 oz candied lemon peel,
  finely chopped
80 g/3 oz self-raising flour
ICING
100 g/4 oz redcurrant jelly
200 g/7 oz icing sugar
1 tablespoon lemon juice
1 tablespoon Maraschino

Grease a 23-cm/9-inch cake
tin. Preheat the oven to
moderately hot (190°C, 375°F,
Gas Mark 5).

Beat the butter with half the
sugar until pale and creamy,
then add the egg yolks one
after another. Mix in the salt,
cinnamon, Maraschino,
breadcrumbs, almonds and
lemon peel. Sift the flour and
fold into the mixture. Whisk
the egg whites until stiff then
whisk in the remaining sugar
until smooth and glossy. Fold
the egg whites into the creamed
mixture, turn into the tin and
bake for 1 hour.

Turn the cake on to a wire
rack to cool. Spread the top
and sides with redcurrant
jelly. Sift the icing sugar and
add the lemon juice and
liqueur. Beat the icing until
smooth, pour on to the cake
and allow to run thickly over
the sides. Smooth the surface
with a palette knife.

Sesame Seed Biscuits

125 g/4½ oz soft margarine
250 g/9 oz castor sugar
1 egg
100 g/4 oz cracked wheat
100 g/3½ oz raisins
120 g/4 oz sesame seeds
2 tablespoons milk
225 g/8 oz plain wholemeal flour
¼ teaspoon grated nutmeg

Grease a baking tray with oil. Preheat the oven to moderately hot (190°C, 375°F, Gas Mark 5).

Beat the margarine with the sugar until pale and creamy. Stir in the egg. Mix the cracked wheat with the raisins, sesame seeds and milk and gradually stir into the mixture. Add the wholemeal flour and nutmeg and stir all the ingredients well together.

Using a teaspoon, place small amounts on the prepared baking tray and flatten slightly. Bake for 10–15 minutes. Remove from the baking tray with a palette knife and leave to cool on a wire rack.

Wholemeal Honey Hearts

450 g/1 lb plain wholemeal flour
¼ teaspoon baking powder
1 teaspoon ground ginger
50 g/2 oz cracked wheat
100 g/4 oz thick honey
150 g/5 oz syrup
150 g/5 oz margarine

Grease a baking tray with margarine.

Sift the flour with the baking powder into a bowl and mix with the ginger and cracked wheat. Warm the honey with the syrup and margarine over a low heat, stirring occasionally until the margarine is completely melted and combined with the honey and syrup. Leave to cool and when lukewarm stir into the flour mixture with a spoon. Knead well, wrap in foil or cling film and leave for 1 hour in the refrigerator.

Preheat the oven to moderate (180°C, 350°F, Gas Mark 4). Roll out the dough on a floured board to 5 mm/¼ inch thick. Cut out heart shapes and place on the prepared baking tray. Bake in the centre of the oven for 12–15 minutes. Remove with a palette knife and leave to cool on a wire rack.

Cook's Tip

Immediately after cooking, the Honey Hearts will be quite hard. If kept for 1–2 days in an airtight tin they will become softer.

Crumble-Based Fruit Tart

18 digestive or wholemeal biscuits
25 g/1 oz castor sugar
¼ teaspoon ground cinnamon
75 g/3 oz butter or margarine, melted
FILLING AND TOPPING
25 g/1 oz cornflour
25 g/1 oz castor sugar
¼ teaspoon vanilla essence
450 ml/¾ pint milk
1 (298-g/10½-oz) can goose-berries
1 (213-g/7½-oz) can peach slices
1 small packet quick-setting jel mix (lemon)

Grease a 23-cm/9-inch flan tin with butter or margarine. Place the biscuits in a poly-thene bag and crush finely with a rolling pin. Mix the biscuit crumbs with the sugar, cinna-mon and melted butter or margarine. Place the mixture in the tin and press down slightly with the back of a spoon. Chill well.

Mix the cornflour with the sugar, vanilla essence and a little of the milk. Heat the remaining milk and pour on to the cornflour mixture. Return to the heat and bring to the boil, stirring continuously. Leave to cool, stirring occa-sionally to prevent a skin forming.

Drain the gooseberries, reserving the juice, and also drain the peaches. Spread the vanilla sauce over the biscuit base and top with the fruit as illustrated. Prepare the glaze using the gooseberry juice, according to the directions on the packet, cool slightly and pour over the tart.

Date Crumble Cake

350 g/12 oz fresh dates
175 g/6 oz plain wholemeal flour
¼ teaspoon salt
100 g/4 oz soft margarine
100 g/4 oz castor sugar
¼ teaspoon vanilla essence
100 g/4 oz medium oatmeal

Grease a 23-cm/9-inch spring-form cake tin with margarine. Preheat the oven to moderate (180°C, 350°F, Gas Mark 4).

Stone the dates and dice finely. Mix the flour with the salt. Beat the margarine with the sugar and vanilla essence until pale and creamy. Gradually add the flour and oatmeal and mix with the fingertips until crumbly.

Spread half the mixture over the base of the cake tin, press down over the base, raising the sides slightly. Spread the dates over this base and crumble the rest of the mixture over the top. Bake for 45–50 minutes. Leave to cool slightly in the tin and serve preferably warm.

Walnut and Banana Bread

150 g/5 oz soft margarine
160 g/5½ oz castor sugar
3 eggs
3 bananas
¼ teaspoon vanilla essence
275 g/10 oz plain wholemeal
    flour
2 teaspoons baking powder
¼ teaspoon salt
100 g/4 oz walnuts, chopped
2 tablespoons milk

Grease a 1-kg/2-lb loaf tin
with margarine. Preheat the
oven to moderate (180°C,
350°F, Gas Mark 4).
  Beat the margarine with the
sugar until pale and creamy
then beat in the eggs. Peel the
bananas and mash with a fork,
or press through a nylon sieve.
Stir the banana purée and
vanilla essence into the
creamed mixture. Mix the
flour and baking powder with
the salt and walnuts. Fold into
the creamed mixture together
with the milk. Turn into the
prepared loaf tin, smooth the
surface and bake for 1¼ hours.
Test with a skewer to make
sure the loaf is cooked through.
  Turn out on to a wire rack
and leave to cool.

Wheatgerm Loaf

60 g/2 oz fresh yeast
750 ml/1¼ pints lukewarm water
2 teaspoons salt
5 tablespoons thick honey
2 tablespoons oil or melted
    margarine
900 g/2 lb wholemeal flour (or
    450 g/1 lb wheatmeal and
    450 g/1 lb wholemeal flour)
150 g/5 oz wheatgerm

Cream the yeast with a little of
the water, add the salt, honey
and oil or melted margarine.
Stir in half the flour. Beat well,
cover and leave to stand in a
warm place for 30 minutes.
Stir in the remaining flour and
the wheatgerm then knead well
to give a smooth elastic dough.
Add a little more flour if the
dough is too wet. Cover and
leave to stand in a warm place
until doubled in size, about 30
minutes.
  Knead the dough thoroughly
again and form into two
loaves. Place on greased
baking trays and leave loosely
covered in a warm place for a
further 15 minutes. Preheat
the oven to moderately hot
(200°C, 400°F, Gas Mark 6).
  Using a sharp knife, lightly
cut a cross on the top of each
loaf and brush with water.
Sprinkle with a little flour and
bake for 50 minutes. Leave the
baked bread to cool on a wire
rack.

Healthy Eating Today

Wholemeal Breakfast Rolls

*500 g / 1 lb plain wholemeal
   flour*
30 g / 1 oz fresh yeast
1 teaspoon sugar
250 ml / 8 fl oz lukewarm water
¼ teaspoon salt
2 tablespoons oil

Lightly grease a baking tray
with margarine.
   Tip the flour into a bowl and
form a well in the centre.
Cream the yeast with the sugar
and a little of the water. Stir
in the remaining water and
pour into the flour. Sprinkle a
little of the flour over this
liquid, cover and leave in a
warm place for 15 minutes,
until frothy.
   Sprinkle the salt around the
edges of the flour, add the oil
to the yeast mixture and knead
all the ingredients together to
make a smooth elastic dough.
Cover again and leave to stand
in a warm place for 30 minutes.
Knead lightly with floured
hands and divide the dough
into 16 equal pieces. Roll each
into a ball, sprinkle with a
little flour and place on the
baking tray. Leave the rolls to
stand in a warm place for a
further 15 minutes. Preheat the
oven to hot (230°C, 450°F,
Gas Mark 8) and bake for
15–20 minutes.

Wholemeal Bread

*400 g / 14 oz strong plain white
   flour*
*400 g / 14 oz plain wholemeal
   flour*
40 g / 1½ oz fresh yeast
500 ml / 17 fl oz lukewarm milk
1 teaspoon salt
7 tablespoons oil

Sift the white flour into a bowl
and mix with the wholemeal
flour. Form a well in the centre.
Cream the yeast with a little of
the milk. Add the remaining
milk and pour into the flour.
Sprinkle with a little of the flour,
cover and leave in a warm
place for 15 minutes, until
frothy. Add the salt and oil
and mix all the ingredients to
a dough. Knead for 5–10
minutes, until smooth and
elastic. Cover and leave to rise
for 30 minutes in a warm
place.
   Knead lightly on a floured
board and form into a loaf.
Sprinkle a baking tray with
flour, place the loaf on it,
cover and leave to stand in a
warm place for a further 30
minutes. Preheat the oven to
moderately hot (190°C, 375°F,
Gas Mark 5). Sprinkle the loaf
with flour and bake for 50–60
minutes.

155

Rum and Raisin Loaf

100 g/4 oz raisins
2 tablespoons rum
500 g/1 lb plain flour
30 g/1 oz fresh yeast
40 g/1½ oz castor sugar
250 ml/8 fl oz lukewarm milk
80 g/3 oz butter, melted
2 eggs
1 teaspoon salt
grated rind of 1 lemon
1 egg yolk, beaten to glaze

Grease a 1-kg/2-lb loaf tin with butter. Mix the raisins with the rum and steep.

Sift the flour into a bowl and make a well in the centre. Cream the yeast with a little of the sugar and milk. Add the remaining milk and pour into the flour. Sprinkle over a little of the flour, cover and leave to stand in a warm place for 15 minutes, until frothy.

Add the rest of the sugar, the melted butter, eggs, salt and lemon rind. Mix to form a soft dough and knead for 5–10 minutes until smooth and elastic. Leave to stand in a warm place until doubled in size, about 30 minutes. Knead in the raisins, place in the loaf tin and leave in a warm place for 30 minutes. Preheat the oven to moderately hot (190°C, 375°F, Gas Mark 5).

Brush with beaten egg yolk and bake for 40–50 minutes.

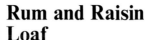

Cook's Tip

Instead of the raisins soaked in rum, knead 100 g/4 oz chopped blanched almonds into the dough and bake as above.

Savoury Bacon Baps

1 kg/2 lb light rye flour
20 g/¾ oz fresh yeast
about 900 ml/1½ pints lukewarm
  water
double quantity starter dough
  (see page 162)
200 g/7 oz bacon
2 teaspoons salt
2 teaspoons caraway seeds
2 teaspoons each caraway seeds
  and sea salt to sprinkle

Place half the flour in a mixing bowl. Cream the yeast with a little of the water, add the remaining water and mix thoroughly into the flour together with the starter dough. Knead until smooth, cover and leave to stand overnight at room temperature.

Preheat the oven to moderately hot (200°C, 400°F, Gas Mark 6). Lightly grill the bacon and chop very finely. Drain on absorbent paper and allow to cool. Mix the salt, caraway seeds, chopped bacon and the rest of the flour into the dough. Knead until smooth.

Divide the dough into six equal pieces and roll out thinly into flat cakes about 25–30 cm/ 10–12 inches in diameter. Brush the tops with water, cut with criss-cross markings and sprinkle with the caraway seeds and sea salt. Place on floured baking trays and bake for 30 minutes.

Flowerpot Loaves

500 g / 1 lb plain flour
30 g / 1 oz fresh yeast
pinch of sugar
175 ml / 6 fl oz lukewarm milk
2 onions
1 clove garlic
50 g / 2 oz butter, melted
2 large eggs, beaten
¼ teaspoon salt
pinch of grated nutmeg
1 teaspoon ground aniseed
¼ teaspoon dried fennel
2 tablespoons dried dill
¼ teaspoon dried rosemary
ground aniseed to sprinkle

Grease two new 10-cm/4-inch earthenware flower pots.

Sift the flour into a bowl and form a well in the centre. Cream the yeast with the sugar and a little of the milk. Stir in the remaining milk and pour into the flour. Sprinkle over a little of the flour, cover and leave in a warm place for 15 minutes, until frothy.

Peel the onions and garlic. Finely chop the onions and crush the garlic. Mix the melted butter with the beaten eggs, salt, nutmeg, aniseed, fennel and dill. Pound the rosemary in a mortar, add to the yeast liquid with the butter mixture, onion and garlic and mix all the ingredients well together. Knead the dough until smooth and elastic. Cover and leave to stand in a warm place until doubled in size, about 30 minutes.

Knead the dough lightly and put half in each of the flowerpots. Leave to stand in a warm place for a further 20 minutes. Preheat the oven to moderately hot (200°C, 400°F, Gas Mark 6).

Brush the surface of the loaves with water and sprinkle lightly with aniseed. Bake for 35–40 minutes.

French Bread

1 kg / 2 lb strong plain flour
40 g / 1½ oz fresh yeast
600 ml / 1 pint lukewarm water
4 teaspoons salt

Sprinkle a large baking tray with flour.

Sift the flour into a bowl and make a well in the centre. Cream the yeast with a little of the water then add the remaining water and pour into the flour. Sprinkle a little of the flour over the liquid, cover and leave to stand in a warm place for 15 minutes. Sprinkle the salt on to the flour and mix all the ingredients to a dough. Knead the dough until smooth and elastic, about 5–10 minutes. Sprinkle well with flour so that the surface does not form a crust, cover and leave to stand for 2–3 hours at room temperature.

Quickly knead the dough again on a floured board and divide into four pieces. Form each piece into a long roll and place on the floured baking tray. Cover and leave to stand in a warm place for a further 30 minutes. Preheat the oven to hot (220°C, 425°F, Gas Mark 7).

Slash the loaves diagonally several times with a fine sharp knife and brush with lukewarm water. Bake for 15 minutes then reduce the oven temperature to moderate (180°C, 350°F, Gas Mark 4) and bake for a further 15–20 minutes.

Country Loaves

Northern Wheel

1 kg/2 lb light rye flour
20 g/¾ oz fresh yeast
about 900 ml/1½ pints lukewarm
* water*
double quantity starter dough
* (see page 162)*
2 teaspoons salt
2 teaspoons each caraway seeds,
* dried fennel and ground*
* aniseed*
milk to glaze

Place half the flour in a mixing
bowl. Cream the yeast with a
little of the water, add the
remaining water and mix
thoroughly into the flour
together with the starter dough.
Knead until smooth, cover and
leave to stand overnight in a
warm place.
   Preheat the oven to very hot
(230°C, 450°F, Gas Mark 8).
Mix the salt, half the spices
and the rest of the flour into
the dough until smooth. Form

one-third of the dough into a
long roll, roll up·to resemble a
snail's shell and place in the
middle of a large floured
baking tray. Form the remaining dough into eight rolls,
20 cm/8 inches in length, place
around the central coil and
slightly roll the end of each
piece, as illustrated. Brush the
surface of the bread with milk
and sprinkle with the rest of
the spices. Bake for 25 minutes
until golden brown.

Fresh Herb Bread

400 g/14 oz strong plain flour
25 g/1 oz fresh yeast
350 ml/12 fl oz lukewarm milk
1 teaspoon salt
1 tablespoon chopped mixed
* herbs, (dill, chives, thyme,*
* parsley)*
1 teaspoon coarsely ground
* black pepper*
milk to glaze

Grease a 1-kg/2-lb loaf tin and
sprinkle with a little flour.
   Sift the flour into a bowl and
make a well in the centre.
Cream the yeast with a little
of the milk then add the
remaining milk and pour into
the flour. Sprinkle over a little
of the flour, cover and leave in
a warm place for 15 minutes,
until frothy. Mix in the salt
and the rest of the flour to
obtain a soft dough. Cover and

leave to stand in a warm place
for a further 1 hour.
   Knead the herbs and pepper
into the dough. Place in the
loaf tin and cut the surface
diagonally with a sharp knife.
Cover and leave the bread to
rise in a warm place for a
further 30 minutes. Preheat
the oven to hot (220°C, 425°F,
Gas Mark 7).
   Brush the loaf with milk and
bake for 35–40 minutes. Cover
with foil if becoming too
brown on top.

Aniseed Marble Bread

PLAIN DOUGH
350 g/12 oz plain flour
20 g/¾ oz fresh yeast
6 tablespoons lukewarm milk
pinch of sugar
50 g/2 oz butter
2 eggs
½ teaspoon salt
RYE DOUGH
350 g/12 oz rye flour
20 g/¾ fresh yeast
6 tablespoons lukewarm milk
pinch of sugar
50 g/2 oz butter
2 eggs
½ teaspoon salt
½ teaspoon ground aniseed
1 tablespoon aniseed to sprinkle

First make the plain dough.
Sift the flour into a bowl and
form a well in the centre.
Cream the yeast with a little of
the milk, add the remaining
milk and pour into the flour.
Add the sugar and sprinkle a
little of the flour over the
surface. Cover and leave to
stand in a warm place for 15
minutes, until frothy. Melt the
butter, stir in the eggs and salt,
add to the yeast liquid and
mix in the flour to make a
dough. Knead the dough until
smooth and elastic. Cover again
and leave in a warm place to
rise for 1 hour.

Make the rye dough in the
same way, using the rye flour.
Incorporate the ground aniseed
into this dough when adding
the butter. Finally leave the
rye dough in a warm place for
1 hour, as above.

Divide both the plain and
rye dough into two pieces.
Lightly knead a piece of each
dough together and shape into
a loaf. Repeat with the remaining two pieces. Place the two
loaves on a floured baking
tray, cover and leave in a warm
place for a further 30 minutes.
Preheat the oven to hot (220°C,
425°F, Gas Mark 7).

Brush the loaves with water,
sprinkle with aniseed and bake
for 30–40 minutes.

Country Loaves

Hearty Peasant Bread

1 kg/2 lb rye flour
20 g/¾ oz fresh yeast
about 600 ml/1 pint lukewarm
   water
double quantity starter dough
   (see page 162)
200 g/7 oz streaky bacon
2 teaspoons salt
200 g/7 oz Emmenthal cheese,
   grated
100 g/3½ oz blanched almonds,
   chopped
2 tablespoons chopped parsley

Place half the flour in a mixing bowl. Cream the yeast with a little of the water, add the remaining water and pour into the flour. Mix in well, together with the starter dough, and knead until smooth. Cover and leave to stand overnight at room temperature.

Lightly grill the bacon and chop very finely. Drain on absorbent paper and allow to cool. Preheat the oven to hot (220°C, 425°F, Gas Mark 7).

Mix the diced bacon, salt, cheese, almonds, parsley and the rest of the flour into the dough and knead until smooth. Form into two round loaves. Place the loaves on a floured baking tray, brush the surface with water, sprinkle with flour and mark a criss-cross pattern on the top. Bake for 20–30 minutes.

French Onion Loaves

1 kg/2 lb rye flour
20 g/¾ oz fresh yeast
about 600 ml/1 pint lukewarm
   water
double quantity starter dough
   (see page 162)
2 teaspoons salt
½ teaspoon freshly ground black
   pepper
generous pinch of ground
   cardamom
4 medium onions
25 g/1 oz butter or margarine

Place half the flour in a mixing bowl. Cream the yeast with a little of the water, add the remaining water and mix thoroughly into the flour with the starter dough. Knead until smooth, cover and leave to stand overnight in a warm place.

Mix the salt and pepper, cardamom and the rest of the flour into the dough and knead thoroughly until smooth.

Peel and finely chop the onions. Brown half the onions in the butter or margarine, drain well and knead into the dough with the raw onion. Form into three loaves about 35 cm/14 inches in length and place on a floured baking tray. Cover and leave to stand in a warm place for a further 15 minutes. Preheat the oven to hot (230°C, 450°F, Gas Mark 8).

Brush the loaves with water, sprinkle with a little flour and with a fine sharp knife cut the surface diagonally several times. Bake for 30 minutes.

Country Loaves

Spiced Flat Cakes

375 g/13 oz rye flour
375 g/13 oz plain wholemeal flour
25 g/1 oz fresh yeast
250 ml/8 fl oz lukewarm water
125 ml/4 fl oz lukewarm milk
1 teaspoon salt
2 teaspoons caraway seeds
2 teaspoons crushed coriander seeds

Grease a baking tray with oil.

Combine the flours in a bowl and form a well in the centre. Cream the yeast with a little of the water. Add the remaining water and the milk then pour into the flour. Sprinkle a little of the flour over the liquid, cover and leave in a warm place for 15 minutes, until frothy.

Mix in all the flour, the salt, caraway and coriander, to make a dough. Knead the dough until smooth, cover and leave to stand in a warm place until doubled in size, about 30 minutes.

Divide the dough into four equal pieces. Roll out each piece to give a large round flat cake. Place on the baking tray, sprinkle with flour and leave to stand in a warm place for 30 minutes. Preheat the oven to hot (230°C, 450°F, Gas Mark 8), and bake for 15–20 minutes, until crisp and golden.

Herb Ring Loaf

50 g/2 oz butter
300 ml/10 fl oz lukewarm water
25 g/1 oz fresh yeast
300 g/11 oz rye flour
300 g/11 oz plain wholemeal flour
2 teaspoons salt
1 tablespoon chopped mixed herbs (marjoram, sage, tarragon, basil)
3 tablespoons chopped parsley

Melt the butter and mix with the water. Cream the yeast with a little of this liquid, add the remaining liquid and leave in a warm place for 15 minutes. Place the rye flour in a bowl and add the wholemeal flour, salt, mixed herbs and parsley. Pour the yeast liquid into the flour and mix to a dough. Knead the dough for about 5 minutes until smooth, cover and leave to rise in a warm place for 30 minutes.

Form the dough into a round flat loaf. Make a hole in the centre of the loaf with a wooden spoon and rotate the spoon to make the hole larger until you have a ring. Place on a greased baking tray, cover and leave in a warm place for 30 minutes.

Preheat the oven to hot (220°C, 425°F, Gas Mark 7). Brush the loaf with water and sprinkle lightly with flour. Make slight slashes in the top of the loaf with a knife and bake for 30 minutes.

161

Strong Ryebread

STARTER DOUGH
1 tablespoon milk
2 tablespoons water
½ teaspoon oil
½ teaspoon dried yeast
1 tablespoon lukewarm water
½ teaspoon castor sugar
1 teaspoon salt
50 g/2 oz strong plain flour
RYEBREAD DOUGH
750 ml/1¼ pints lukewarm water
750 g/1 lb 10 oz coarse rye flour
250 g/9 oz wheaten flour
2 teaspoons salt

First make the starter dough. Combine the milk, 2 tablespoons water and the oil in a saucepan and bring to the boil. Allow to cool until lukewarm. Blend the yeast with 1 tablespoon lukewarm water and the sugar and leave for 5 minutes. Add to the milk mixture with the salt. Stir this liquid into the flour until well blended then cover and leave to stand for 12–18 hours.

The following day, mix the starter dough with 500 ml/ 17 fl oz of the lukewarm wate Mix the rye flour with the wheaten flour in a large warmed bowl. Make a well in the centre of the flours and pour in the starter dough. Stir half the flour into the starter dough until a thick flowing dough is formed. Cover the bowl with a tea towel and leave to rise overnight in a warm place.

The following day add the remaining lukewarm water and the salt. Mix the rest of the flour into the dough and knead until firm and well bound together. Form the dough into a ball and place in a warmed, lightly floured bowl. Cover it with a tea towel and leave in a warm place to rise for 3 hours.

Line a large baking tray with foil. With floured hands shape the dough into a flat round loaf. Place on the baking tray and once again leave to rise at room temperature for 1½–2 hours. During this time brush the top of the loaf three or four times with lukewarm water so that no crust forms. Cut criss-cross patterns on the top of the risen loaf with a sharp knife. Preheat the oven to moderately hot (200°C, 400°F, Gas Mark 6) and bake the loaf on the bottom shelf for 2 hours.

Turn off the oven, remove the bread, brush with cold water and return to the oven for a few minutes to dry.

Cook's Tip

Rye flour can be bought in most healthfood shops. Bread made from rye flour has an agreeable taste and will keep fresh for longer than ordinary bread.

Savoury Veal Loaf

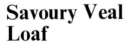

1 (283-g/10-oz) packet bread
    mix
1 tablespoon milk to glaze
FILLING
1 (675-g/1½-lb) fillet of veal
1 teaspoon salt
1 teaspoon paprika pepper
2 tablespoons oil
1 medium onion
4 tablespoons canned green
    peppercorns
2–3 tablespoons made mustard
pinch of dried rosemary
pinch of dried sage

First prepare the filling.
Season the meat with the salt
and paprika. Heat the oil in a
pan and fry the meat for 10
minutes, turning frequently.
Leave to cool.

Peel and chop the onion
finely. Drain the green peppercorns and chop finely. Preheat

the oven to moderately hot
(200°C, 400°F, Gas Mark 6).

Mix the mustard, rosemary
and sage with the chopped
onion and peppercorns, then
spread this mixture over the
meat. Prepare the bread mix
according to the instructions
on the packet and roll out to
a rectangle large enough to
cover the meat. Place the meat
on the dough and fold the
dough over carefully to
completely cover it. Press the
edges together firmly to seal.

Place the loaf on a greased
baking tray with the join of the
dough underneath. Brush with
milk and bake for 30 minutes.
Serve either warm or cold.

Savoury Chicken Loaves

YEAST DOUGH
500 g/1 lb rye flour
15 g/½ oz fresh yeast
450 ml/¾ pint lukewarm water
1 quantity starter dough (see
    page 162)
1 teaspoon salt
1 egg yolk, beaten to glaze
caraway seeds to sprinkle
FILLING
4 (175-g/6-oz) chicken breast
    portions
20 g/1 oz butter
4 shallots
50 g/2 oz button mushrooms
225 g/8 oz sausagemeat
1 tablespoon chopped herbs
1 egg yolk
1 tablespoon single cream
pinch each of salt, pepper,
    ground coriander and allspice

Place the flour in a bowl and
form a well. Cream the yeast

with a little of the water. Add
the remaining water and mix
into the flour with the starter
dough and salt. Knead until
smooth, cover and leave overnight at room temperature.

Season the chicken, cook in
the butter then cool. Preheat
the oven to moderately hot
(200°C, 400°F, Gas Mark 6).

Finely chop the shallots and
mushrooms. Mix with the
sausagemeat, herbs, egg yolk,
cream, seasoning and spices.
Spread this around each of the
chicken portions. Lightly knead
the dough and roll out to
5 mm/¼ inch thick. Cut into
four equal-sized rounds and
place a coated chicken portion
on each. Fold the dough over
the chicken and press the edges
together to seal. Place on
a floured baking tray, brush
with beaten egg yolk and
sprinkle with caraway seeds.
Bake for 30 minutes and serve
hot or cold.

Rolls and Crescents

Poppy Seed Rolls

500 g/1 lb plain flour
1 teaspoon salt
30 g/1 oz fresh yeast
250 ml/8 fl oz lukewarm milk
50 g/2 oz butter or margarine
1 egg
pinch each of pepper and grated
* nutmeg*
GLAZE
1 egg yolk
1 tablespoon milk
2 tablespoons poppy seeds

Sift the flour and salt into a
bowl and make a well in the
centre. Cream the yeast with a
little of the milk, add the
remaining milk and pour into
the flour. Sprinkle a little of the
flour over the liquid, cover and
leave in a warm place for 15
minutes, until frothy.

Melt the butter or margarine
and mix with the egg, pepper
and nutmeg. Add these ingredients to the bowl and mix

everything to a dough. Knead
until smooth and elastic. Cover
and leave the dough to rise
until doubled in size.

Grease two baking trays.
Lightly knead the dough, break
off pieces of approximately
40 g/1½ oz, and with floured
hands shape these into balls.
Place them on the baking
trays and press to flatten
slightly. Leave the rolls to rise
in a warm place for a further
20 minutes. Preheat the oven
to hot (230°C, 450°F, Gas
Mark 8).

Beat the egg yolk with the
milk. Brush the rolls with this
and sprinkle with a few poppy
seeds. Cut a cross in the top of
each roll and bake for 15–20
minutes.

Crusty Rye Rolls

500 g/1 lb rye flour
15 g/½ oz fresh yeast
about 450 ml/¾ pint lukewarm
* water*
1 quantity starter dough (see
* page 162)*
1 teaspoon salt

Place half the flour in a bowl.
Cream the yeast with a little of
the water then add the remaining water and mix thoroughly
into the flour, together with
the starter dough. Knead until
smooth, cover the dough and
leave overnight in a warm
place.

Preheat the oven to hot
(230°C, 450°F, Gas Mark 8).
Mix the remaining flour with
the salt and work into the
dough. Knead thoroughly
until smooth. Divide the dough
into 16 pieces and form into
round rolls. Arrange the rolls
on greased baking trays and

brush with water. Dust with
sifted flour and make a cut in
each with a knife. Bake the
rolls for 20–25 minutes.

Dinner Rolls

500 g/1 lb strong plain white
* flour*
30 g/1 oz fresh yeast
250 ml/8 fl oz lukewarm milk
pinch of sugar
1 teaspoon salt
1 egg
1 egg yolk, beaten to glaze
sesame seeds and poppy seeds to
* sprinkle*

Sift the flour into a bowl and
make a well in the centre.
Cream the yeast with a little of
the milk and the sugar. Add the
remaining milk and pour into
the flour. Sprinkle a little of the
flour over the liquid, cover and
leave in a warm place for 15
minutes, until frothy.

Sprinkle the salt on to the
edges of the flour, add the egg
to the yeast liquid and mix all
together to form a dough.
Knead the dough until it is
smooth and elastic, about
5–10 minutes. Cover and leave
to rise in a warm place until
doubled in size.

Divide the dough into small
portions and form into 20-cm/
8-inch long rolls, about 2·5 cm/
1 inch in diameter. From these
shape rolls as shown in the
illustration. Place the rolls
on greased baking trays, cover
and leave to rise in a warm
place for 20 minutes. Preheat
the oven to hot (230°C, 450°F,
Gas Mark 8).

Brush the rolls with beaten
egg yolk, and sprinkle some
with sesame seeds and some
with poppy seeds. Bake the
rolls for 10–15 minutes, until
golden brown.

Rolls and Crescents

Milk Crescents

500 g / 1 lb plain flour
30 g / 1 oz fresh yeast
250 ml / 8 fl oz lukewarm milk
30 g / 1 oz butter or margarine
1 teaspoon sugar
½ teaspoon salt
1 egg
1 egg yolk, beaten to glaze

Sift the flour into a bowl and make a well in the centre. Cream the yeast with a little of the milk, add the remaining milk and then pour into the flour. Sprinkle a little of the flour over the yeast liquid, cover and leave in a warm place for 15 minutes, until frothy.

Melt the butter or margarine and mix with the sugar, salt and egg. Add to the yeast liquid and flour and mix all together to give a dough. Knead until smooth and elastic then leave in a warm place until doubled in size.

Divide the dough into pieces weighing approximately 50 g / 2 oz and shape into balls. Roll out each into a triangular shape, with sides approximately 15 cm / 6 inches long. Press the point of each triangle firmly on to a baking tray and, starting at the other end, roll up with both hands. Finally seal the point of the triangle with a little beaten egg yolk. Curve each roll into a crescent shape, arrange on a baking tray and brush with beaten egg yolk. Cover and leave to rise for 15–20 minutes in a warm place. Preheat the oven to hot (230°C, 450°F, Gas Mark 8).

Bake the crescents for 10–15 minutes until golden brown and serve fresh from the oven.

Poppy Seed Plaits

500 g / 1 lb plain flour
30 g / 1 oz fresh yeast
250 ml / 8 fl oz lukewarm water
1 teaspoon salt
1 egg
poppy seeds to sprinkle

Sift the flour into a bowl and make a well in the centre. Cream the yeast with a little of the water, add the remaining water and pour into the flour. Sprinkle over a little of the flour, cover and leave in a warm place for 15 minutes, until frothy.

Sprinkle the salt on the flour, add the egg to the yeast liquid and mix the ingredients to a dough. If it is too stiff, add a little more lukewarm water. Knead until smooth and elastic. Cover and leave to rise in a warm place, until doubled in size, about 30 minutes.

Divide the mixture into 50-g/2-oz pieces. Form three long thin strands from each piece, about 15 cm/6 inches in length, and weave into small plaits. Brush these plaits with water and sprinkle with poppy seeds. Arrange on a greased baking tray, cover and leave to rise in a warm place for about 15 minutes. Preheat the oven to hot (230°C, 450°F, Gas Mark 8).

Bake the poppy seed plaits for 10–20 minutes and serve fresh from the oven.

Croissants

550 g/1 lb 2 oz plain flour
30 g/1 oz fresh yeast
250 ml/8 fl oz lukewarm milk
225 g/8 oz butter
1 egg
1 teaspoon salt
1 egg yolk, beaten to glaze

Sift 500 g/1 lb flour into a bowl and make a well. Cream the yeast with the milk, pour into the flour, cover and leave in a warm place for 15 minutes. Mix in 50 g/2 oz melted butter, the egg and salt, then knead until a smooth, elastic dough. Cover and leave in a warm place for 1 hour.

Knead lightly and roll out to a 20 × 35-cm/8 × 14-inch rectangle. Work the rest of the flour into the remaining butter and chill. Divide into thirds and mark the pastry dough into three lengthways. Dot one-third of the butter over the top two-thirds of the pastry, leaving a border. Fold the bottom third of pastry over the middle third and the top third over that. Press the edges together, give one turn in a clockwise direction and then roll out to the original size. Repeat this folding and rolling process twice more with the remaining butter, then twice without any butter. Chill for 30 minutes between each rolling.

Finally roll out the dough to a 50-cm/20-inch square. Cut into sixteen 12·5-cm/5-inch squares and roll up each, starting from one corner to the opposite corner. Place on baking trays, brush with egg yolk and leave in a warm place for 30 minutes.

Preheat the oven to hot (220°C, 425°F, Gas Mark 7). Bake the croissants for 5 minutes then reduce to 190°C, 375°F, Gas Mark 5 for a further 15 minutes.

Brioches

500 g/1 lb plain flour
30 g/1 oz fresh yeast
6 tablespoons lukewarm milk
1 teaspoon castor sugar
200 g/7 oz butter
4 eggs
½ teaspoon salt
1 egg yolk, beaten to glaze

Grease 20 small brioche or patty tins with butter.

Sift the flour into a bowl and make a well in the centre. Cream the yeast with a little of the milk, add the remaining milk and the sugar. Pour into the well in the flour, sprinkle a little of the flour over, cover and leave in a warm place for 15 minutes.

Melt the butter, cool slightly and mix with the eggs and salt. Beat into the yeast mixture with the rest of the flour, kneading with your hand to give a smooth dough. Leave covered in a warm place for 30 minutes.

Knead lightly, take three-quarters of the dough and shape into approximately 20 small balls. Place in the greased tins. Make 20 smaller pear-shaped pieces out of the remaining dough. Make a small indentation in the dough in the tins and place the smaller pieces of dough on top, with the slightly elongated end in the indentation. Brush the brioches with beaten egg yolk and leave to rise in a warm place for 15 minutes. Preheat the oven to hot (220°C, 425°F, Gas Mark 7).

Bake the brioches for about 15 minutes, until well risen and golden brown. Remove from the oven and allow to cool on a wire rack.

Crispy Fried Cakes

Saffron Plaits

4 saffron strands
250 ml/8 fl oz hot milk
500 g/1 lb plain flour
50 g/2 oz castor sugar
¼ teaspoon salt
grated rind of ½ lemon
30 g/1 oz fresh yeast
120 g/4 oz margarine
2 eggs
100 g/4 oz castor sugar to
    sprinkle
oil to deep fry

Steep the saffron in the hot
milk overnight.

Sift the flour into a bowl
then add the sugar, salt and
lemon rind. Mix these dry
ingredients together and make
a well in the centre. Strain the
milk and reheat to lukewarm.
Cream the yeast with a little of
this lukewarm milk, add the
remaining milk and pour it
into the well in the flour.
Sprinkle a little of the flour

over the yeast liquid, cover
and leave in a warm place for
15 minutes.

Melt the margarine and mix
with the eggs. Add this to the
yeast liquid and beat in the dry
ingredients to form a soft
dough. Knead on a well-
floured board for 5–10 minutes,
until smooth and elastic. Cover
and leave in a warm place for
30 minutes.

Knead the dough lightly and
divide into four pieces. Divide
each of these pieces into four
and roll out into 15–20-cm/
6–8-inch strips. Plait these
four strips together, cover and
leave to rise in a warm place
for 15–20 minutes.

Heat the oil for frying to
149°C/300°F and fry the
plaits, turning over at least
once, for 10 minutes, until
golden brown and cooked
through. Drain on absorbent
paper and coat one side with
sugar while still hot.

Sugared Knots

125 g/4½ oz soft margarine
125 g/4½ oz castor sugar
pinch of salt
3 eggs
1 tablespoon rum
450 g/1 lb plain flour
2 teaspoons baking powder
COATING
100 g/4 oz castor sugar
25 g/1 oz vanilla sugar
oil or fat to deep fry

Beat the margarine, sugar, salt
and eggs together thoroughly,
until smooth. Mix in the rum.
Sift the flour and baking
powder together over the
mixture and fold in thoroughly.
Knead well, wrap in foil or
cling film and leave in the
refrigerator for 30 minutes.
Heat the oil for frying to
182°C/360°F.

Roll out the dough on a
floured surface to 5 mm/¼ inch
thick and cut into 20 × 1·5-cm/

8 × ¾-inch strips. Knot each
strip tightly. Fry four at a
time in the deep oil for 5
minutes, turning once with a
draining spoon. Drain on
absorbent paper.

Mix the sugar and vanilla
sugar together and use to coat
the warm knots.

Tunisian Honey Rings

3 eggs
3 tablespoons oil
3 tablespoons orange juice
grated rind of 1 large orange
50 g / 2 oz castor sugar
300 g / 11 oz plain flour
1 teaspoon baking powder
SYRUP
300 ml / ½ pint cold water
2 tablespoons lemon juice
275 g / 10 oz granulated sugar
100 g / 4 oz thick honey
oil to deep fry

Whisk the eggs with the oil, orange juice, 1 teaspoon orange rind and the sugar until frothy. Sift the flour with the baking powder and add a spoonful at a time to the whisked mixture. Beat well, cover and leave to stand for 45 minutes.

Heat the water and lemon juice with the sugar, stirring continuously until the sugar has dissolved. Bring to the boil and simmer for 5 minutes. Add the honey and remaining orange rind and simmer the syrup gently for a further 5 minutes. Keep warm while cooking the doughnut rings.

Heat the oil for frying to 182°C/360°F. Divide the dough into 12 pieces. Using floured hands, form each piece into a circle 7·5 cm/3 inches in diameter. Make a hole in the centre, and enlarge it using a wooden spoon until about 3·5 cm/1½ inches in diameter. Fry three rings at a time in the hot oil for 5 minutes until golden brown, turning once. Drain the rings on absorbent paper.

Pick up each ring on a fork while still warm and dip into the syrup for a few minutes, allowing the syrup to soak in. Serve immediately.

Jam Rosettes

150 g / 6 oz soft margarine
100 g / 4 oz castor sugar
2 eggs
50 g / 2 oz ground almonds
1 teaspoon ground cinnamon
125 ml / 4 fl oz soured cream
500 g / 1 lb plain flour
1 egg white, beaten
icing sugar to sprinkle
200 g / 7 oz redcurrant jelly
oil or fat to deep fry

Mix the margarine with the sugar and eggs until light. Stir in the ground almonds, cinnamon, soured cream and a little of the sifted flour, until well mixed. Finally add the remaining flour. Wrap the mixture in foil or cling film and leave in the refrigerator for 1 hour.

Heat the oil for frying to 182°C/360°F. Roll out the dough thinly on a floured board, and cut out fluted circles measuring 6 cm/2½ inches in diameter. Cut notches into the edge of these as illustrated. Brush them in the centre with beaten egg white, and lay three rounds one on top of the other. Using the handle of a wooden spoon, shape a small well in the centre. During cooking, each layer rises to make a rosette shape.

Place two or three rosettes in the hot oil and fry for 4–5 minutes, until golden brown, turning once. Drain them well on absorbent paper and sprinkle with sifted icing sugar. Fill the centres of the rosettes with redcurrant jelly.

Country Plum Strudel

PASTRY
15 g/½ oz lard
6 tablespoons lukewarm water
1 egg
pinch of salt
250 g/9 oz plain flour
FILLING
1 kg/2 lb plums
140 g/5 oz butter
100 g/4 oz fresh white
  breadcrumbs
75 g/3 oz castor sugar
icing sugar to sprinkle

Melt the fat and beat with the water, egg and salt. Sift the flour on top and mix everything together to a smooth dough. Roll the dough into a ball, return to the bowl, cover and leave to stand for 1 hour.

Roll out the pastry as thinly as possible on a large floured cloth. Finally stretch the pastry with your hands, working from the middle outwards until it is paper thin. If the pastry tears join it together immediately. Put the pastry back on the cloth. Preheat the oven to moderately hot (200°C, 400°F, Gas Mark 6).

Wash the plums and quarter them, removing the stones. Melt the butter and put 2 tablespoons of it to one side. Mix the rest with the breadcrumbs and spread this over two-thirds of the pastry, leaving the bottom third uncovered. Arrange the plums over the top of the bread-crumbs and sprinkle with the castor sugar. Spread a little butter on the uncovered third of the pastry and, lifting the cloth, roll the pastry up, starting from the covered side. Place the strudel on a greased baking tray and brush with the remaining butter. Bake for 40 minutes and dust with icing sugar before serving warm with cream.

Cook's Tip

To make Apple Strudel, as illustrated left, substitute 675 g/1½ lb cooking apples, peeled, cored and sliced, and 50 g/2 oz raisins, for the plums.

Nut Strudel

1 (368-g/13-oz) packet frozen
*   puff pastry*
FILLING
2 egg yolks
80 g/3 oz castor sugar
50 g/2 oz butter
200 g/7 oz walnuts, finely
*   chopped or ground*
75 g/3 oz biscuit crumbs
½ teaspoon ground cinnamon
grated rind of ½ lemon
1 tablespoon rum
50 g/2 oz raisins
1–2 tablespoons milk
1 egg yolk, beaten to glaze

Allow the pastry to thaw at
room temperature for 1 hour.

To make the filling, whisk
the egg yolks with the sugar
until thick and creamy. Melt
the butter and mix it with the
walnuts, biscuit crumbs,
cinnamon, lemon rind, rum
and raisins. Stir into the
whisked eggs, adding just

enough milk to make a thick
mixture.

Roll out three-quarters of
the pastry thinly to a 25 × 30-
cm/10 × 12-inch rectangle.
Place the filling down the
centre of the pastry. Brush the
edges with beaten egg yolk
and fold the pastry over the
filling, sealing the edges
together. Place on a dampened
baking tray with the join
underneath. Brush with egg
yolk. Roll out the remaining
pastry and cut into strips with
a pastry cutter. Arrange in a
lattice pattern on top of the
pastry and brush with egg yolk.
Leave the strudel to stand for
15 minutes.

Preheat the oven to hot
(220°C, 425°F, Gas Mark 7).
Bake the strudel for 35–45
minutes, covering the top with
foil if it becomes too brown.

Apple Fritters

75 g/3 oz castor sugar
¾ teaspoon ground cinnamon
2 tablespoons rum
4 large ripe apples
oil or fat to deep fry
BATTER
125 g/5 oz plain flour
½ teaspoon baking powder
pinch of salt
2 eggs, separated
1 tablespoon olive oil
9 tablespoons light ale
TO SPRINKLE
100 g/4 oz castor sugar
1 teaspoon ground cinnamon

Mix the sugar and cinnamon
with the rum in a shallow dish.
Peel the apples, remove the
cores and cut into 1-cm/½-inch
thick slices. Toss the apple
slices in the sugar mixture.
Cover and leave for 30
minutes, turning once or twice
to allow the flavour to be
absorbed.

Sift the flour and baking
powder together and mix with
the salt, egg yolks and oil,
beating until smooth. Stir in
the beer. Whisk the egg whites
until stiff and fold into the
batter.

Heat the oil or fat for frying
to 182°C/360°F. Coat the
apple slices in the batter and
fry in the hot oil for 8–10
minutes, turning them once
during the cooking time, until
golden brown. Drain on
absorbent paper and sprinkle
with the mixed sugar and
cinnamon while still hot. Serve
warm.

Sweet Plum Rounds

YEAST DOUGH
500 g/1 lb plain flour
30 g/1 oz fresh yeast
80 g/3 oz castor sugar
250 ml/8 fl oz lukewarm milk
50 g/2 oz butter, melted
grated rind of ½ lemon
1 egg, beaten
pinch of salt
1 egg yolk, beaten to glaze
FILLING
500 g/1 lb curd or cream cheese
50 g/2 oz butter, softened
200 g/7 oz castor sugar
2 eggs, separated
1 tablespoon cornflour
1 tablespoon rum
250 g/9 oz ground poppy seeds
80 g/3 oz sugar
1 tablespoon fresh white
 breadcrumbs
250 ml/8 fl oz milk
250 g/9 oz stewed plums, puréed

Make up the dough following the method for Dresden Slices (see page 178), and adding the lemon rind with the melted butter.

Mix the cheese, butter, castor sugar, egg yolks, cornflour and rum together. Whisk the egg whites until stiff and fold into this mixture.

Stir the poppy seeds, sugar, breadcrumbs and milk together and bring to the boil. Leave to cool.

Divide the yeast into 50-g/ 2-oz pieces. Shape into rounds, pinching up the edges to form a side, and brush with beaten egg yolk. Put 4 small spoonfuls of the cheese mixture and 4 small spoonfuls of the poppy mixture alternately into each round, and a spoonful of puréed plum in the centre. Cover and leave to rise for 10 minutes. Preheat the oven to moderately hot (200°C, 400°F, Gas Mark 6) and bake the rounds for 20–25 minutes.

Creamy Raisin Squares

YEAST DOUGH
350 g/12 oz plain flour
20 g/¾ oz fresh yeast
50 g/2 oz castor sugar
6 tablespoons lukewarm milk
50 g/2 oz margarine, melted
2 eggs
pinch of salt
TOPPING
300 ml/½ pint double cream
3 eggs, separated
50 g/2 oz castor sugar
1 tablespoon semolina
75 g/3 oz raisins

Sift the flour into a bowl and make a well in the centre. Cream the yeast with a little of the sugar and the milk. Pour into the well in the flour and sprinkle over a little of the flour. Cover and leave in a warm place for 15 minutes, until frothy.

Add the remaining sugar, the melted margarine, eggs and salt to the mixture, and beat all the ingredients to a dough. Knead until smooth and elastic on a lightly floured board. Cover and leave the dough to rise for 1 hour. Knead lightly again then roll out the dough to fit a greased 23 × 33-cm/9 × 13-inch Swiss roll tin. Preheat the oven to moderately hot (200°C, 400°F, Gas Mark 6).

Mix the cream, egg yolks, sugar and semolina together. Whisk the egg whites until stiff and fold in the raisins. Fold the egg whites into the cream mixture and spread this over the dough.

Bake for 20–25 minutes. Cut into squares and eat preferably warm.

Country Butter Cake

450 g/1 lb plain flour
40 g/1½ oz fresh yeast
250 ml/8 fl oz lukewarm milk
225 g/8 oz castor sugar
225 g/8 oz butter
pinch of salt
1 egg, beaten
1 teaspoon ground cinnamon

Grease two baking trays with butter or margarine.

Sift the flour into a bowl and make a well in the centre. Cream the yeast with a little of the milk and 1 teaspoon sugar and pour into the well. Sprinkle over a little of the flour, cover and leave in a warm place for 15 minutes, until frothy.

Melt half the butter and place the remaining butter in the refrigerator. Add 50 g/2 oz sugar, the salt, egg, melted butter and remaining milk to the yeast mixture and beat with the flour to form a dough. Knead on a floured surface until smooth and elastic. Leave to rise for 1 hour in a warm place.

Preheat the oven to hot (220°C, 425°F, Gas Mark 7). Roll out the dough to fit two 25 × 30-cm/10 × 12-inch baking trays. Make small wells in the surface of the dough and into these put the remaining butter, cut into flakes. Mix the rest of the sugar with the cinnamon and sprinkle over the cakes. Bake for 25 minutes, leave the cakes to cool and then cut into slices.

Butter Cream Sandwich Fingers

BISCUIT MIXTURE
500 g/1 lb plain flour
15 g/½ oz fresh yeast
175 g/6 oz castor sugar
250 ml/8 fl oz lukewarm milk
90 g/3½ oz butter
1 egg
¼ teaspoon grated lemon rind
100 g/4 oz almonds, chopped
1 tablespoon cold milk
BUTTER CREAM
75 g/3 oz unsalted butter
175 g/6 oz icing sugar
¼ teaspoon vanilla essence

Sift the flour into a bowl and make a well in the centre. Cream the yeast with 1 tablespoon of sugar and 2 tablespoons of the milk. Pour into the well in the flour, sprinkle with a little of the flour and leave in a warm place for 15 minutes, until frothy.

Melt 50 g/2 oz butter in the remaining warm milk and add to the bowl with the egg, 50 g/2 oz sugar and the lemon rind. Form into a dough and knead. Spread out on a greased baking tray and leave to rise for 1–1½ hours.

Preheat the oven to moderately hot (200°C, 400°F, Gas Mark 6).

Melt the remaining butter, and stir in the remaining sugar and the almonds. Mix in the tablespoon of milk, cool, then spread over the dough. Bake for 40 minutes, cool and cut into fingers.

Split each finger in half horizontally through the centre. Cream the butter with the sifted icing sugar and vanilla essence until light and fluffy. Sandwich together the fingers with this butter cream.

177

Marbled Crumble Cake

YEAST DOUGH
350 g/12 oz plain flour
20 g/¾ oz fresh yeast
50 g/2 oz castor sugar
125 ml/4 fl oz lukewarm milk
50 g/2 oz margarine, melted
2 eggs
pinch of salt
FILLINGS
250 ml/8 fl oz milk
20 g/¾ oz margarine
grated rind of ½ lemon
30 g/1 oz semolina
100 g/4 oz ground poppy seeds
50 g/2 oz sugar
1 egg
1 tablespoon rum
¼ teaspoon ground cinnamon
250 g/9 oz curd or cream cheese
3 tablespoons milk
1 egg, separated
100 g/4 oz castor sugar
250 g/9 oz cherry jam
1 tablespoon rum

CRUMBLE TOPPING
75 g/3 oz butter, melted
175 g/6 oz plain flour
90 g/3½ oz castor sugar

Make the dough as for Dresden Slices (see right) and line a greased 23 × 33-cm/9 × 13-inch Swiss roll tin.

Bring the 250 ml/8 fl oz milk to the boil with the margarine, lemon rind and semolina, and leave for 5 minutes. Mix in the poppy seeds, sugar, egg, rum and cinnamon.

Mix together the cheese, milk, egg yolk and sugar. Whisk the egg white until stiff and fold in. Mix the jam and rum together.

Rub the melted butter into the flour and sugar until crumbly. Spread spoonfuls of the poppy seed, cheese and jam mixtures over the dough, and top with the crumble. Leave for 15 minutes then bake in a hot oven (220°C, 425°F, Gas Mark 7) for 20–30 minutes.

Dresden Slices

YEAST DOUGH
225 g/8 oz plain flour
15 g/½ oz fresh yeast
25 g/1 oz castor sugar
6 tablespoons lukewarm milk
25 g/1 oz margarine, melted
1 egg, beaten
pinch of salt
FILLING
350 g/12 oz curd or cream cheese
100 g/4 oz castor sugar
1 egg
1 tablespoon plain flour
grated rind of 1 lemon
TOPPING
100 g/4 oz butter
100 g/4 oz castor sugar
1 tablespoon plain flour
2 eggs
100 g/4 oz flaked almonds

Sift the flour into a bowl and make a well in the centre. Cream the yeast with a little of the sugar and the milk. Pour into the well and sprinkle the surface with a little of the flour. Cover the bowl and leave for 15 minutes, until frothy. Add the remaining sugar, the melted margarine, egg and salt, and beat all the ingredients until a dough is formed. Knead lightly, cover and leave to rise for 1 hour.

Mix the cheese with the sugar, egg, flour and lemon rind, beating until light and fluffy.

Lightly knead the dough and roll out to line a greased 33 × 23-cm/13 × 9-inch Swiss roll tin. Spread the cheese filling over it evenly.

Preheat the oven to moderately hot (200°C, 400°F, Gas Mark 6). Beat the butter and sugar until creamy. Add the flour and the eggs, one at a time. Spread over the cheese filling and finally sprinkle with the almonds. Bake the cake for 30–40 minutes. Allow to cool slightly then cut into slices.

Swiss Plum Slice

YEAST DOUGH
350 g/12 oz plain flour
20 g/¾ oz fresh yeast
6 tablespoons lukewarm milk
50 g/2 oz butter
50 g/2 oz castor sugar
pinch of salt
2 eggs
TOPPING
1 kg/2 lb plums
50 g/2 oz sugar crystals
½ teaspoon ground cinnamon

Sift the flour into a bowl and make a well in the centre. Cream the yeast with the milk and pour into the well. Sprinkle the surface with a little flour, cover and leave in a warm place for 15 minutes, until frothy.

Melt the butter but do not let it get hot. Add the butter to the flour with the sugar, salt and eggs and beat everything to a dough. Knead lightly, cover and leave to rise for 1 hour.

Wash the plums, remove the stones and cut lengthways into quarters. Knead the dough lightly and roll out to fit a greased 33 × 23-cm/13 × 9-inch Swiss roll tin. Prick all over with a fork. Arrange the plums in overlapping rows on the dough and leave to rise for a further 15 minutes. Preheat the oven to moderately hot (200°C, 400°F, Gas Mark 6).

Bake for 20–30 minutes and sprinkle with the sugar and cinnamon while still warm.

Apple Crumble Cake

YEAST DOUGH
225 g/8 oz plain flour
15 g/½ oz fresh yeast
25 g/1 oz castor sugar
6 tablespoons lukewarm milk
25 g/1 oz butter, melted
1 egg
pinch of salt
grated rind of 1 lemon
TOPPING
1 kg/2 lb apples
350 g/12 oz plain flour
200 g/7 oz sugar
25 g/1 oz vanilla sugar
200 g/7 oz butter, cut into flakes
100 g/3½ oz currants

Sift the flour into a bowl and make a well in the centre. Cream the yeast with a little of the sugar and the milk. Pour into the well and sprinkle the surface with a little of the flour. Cover and leave in a warm place for 15 minutes, until frothy. Add the remaining sugar, the melted butter, egg, salt and lemon rind, and mix all the ingredients together to a dough. Knead lightly and leave for 1 hour.

Peel, core and slice the apples. Lightly knead the dough and roll out to fit a greased 23 × 33-cm/9 × 13-inch Swiss roll tin. Arrange the apple slices in overlapping rows on the dough. Preheat the oven to moderately hot (200°C, 400°F, Gas Mark 6).

Sift the flour into a bowl and add the sugar and vanilla sugar. Rub in the butter with the fingertips until crumbly. Spread the crumble over the apples, sprinkling with the currants.

Bake the cake for 25–35 minutes. Leave to cool then cut into slices.

179

Hazelnut Stollen

500 g / 1 lb plain flour
30 g / 1 oz fresh yeast
70 g / 2¼ oz castor sugar
250 ml / 8 fl oz lukewarm milk
100 g / 3½ oz margarine, melted
1 egg
½ teaspoon salt
grated rind of ½ lemon
FILLING AND ICING
100 g / 4 oz ground almonds
100 g / 4 oz soft brown sugar
100 g / 4 oz ground hazelnuts
2 egg whites, lightly beaten
2 tablespoons rum
¼ teaspoon ground cinnamon
1 egg yolk, beaten to glaze
120 g / 4½ oz icing sugar, sifted
1–2 tablespoons lemon juice
50 g / 2 oz toasted hazelnuts

Sift the flour into a bowl and
form a well. Cream the yeast
with a little of the sugar and
the milk. Pour into the well,
cover and leave for 15 minutes,
until frothy. Add the remaining

sugar, the margarine, egg, salt
and lemon rind and mix to a
dough. Knead lightly then
leave to rise for 1 hour.

Mix the almonds, sugar,
hazelnuts, egg whites, rum and
cinnamon. Knead the dough
lightly and roll out to a 45-cm/
18-inch square. Spread over the
filling. Brush the sides with egg
yolk and roll up. Place on a
greased baking tray, brush with
egg and leave for 15 minutes.
Preheat the oven to 220°C,
425°F, Gas Mark 7.

Bake the stollen for 30–40
minutes. Ice with the sugar and
lemon juice and sprinkle with
chopped hazelnuts.

Note To make the variation on
the jacket, roll the dough into
two oblongs. Spread each with
filling, roll up and twist together
into a ring. Place in a ring tin
and cook as above. Ice and
sprinkle with flaked almonds.

Bohemian Plait

500 g / 1 lb plain flour
30 g / 1 oz fresh yeast
60 g / 2 oz castor sugar
250 ml / 8 fl oz lukewarm milk
100 g / 4 oz margarine
pinch of salt
50 g / 2 oz raisins
1 egg yolk, beaten to glaze
2 tablespoons sugar crystals to
  sprinkle

Sift the flour into a bowl and
make a well in the centre.
Cream the yeast with a little
of the sugar and the milk and
pour into the well. Sprinkle the
surface with a little of the
flour. Cover and leave in a
warm place for 15 minutes,
until frothy.

Melt the margarine, add it
to the bowl with the remaining
sugar, the salt and raisins, and
beat all the ingredients to a
dough. Knead on a lightly
floured surface, then cover and

leave to rise for 1 hour.

Halve the dough. Divide one
half into three 35-cm/14-inch
strips and use to make a plait.
Place on a greased baking tray.
From two-thirds of the
remaining dough, make an-
other smaller plait. From the
remaining dough, make two
strips and form a twist. Brush
the larger of the plaits with
beaten egg yolk, place the
smaller one on top and brush
this. Finally place the twist
on top and brush with beaten
egg yolk. Sprinkle with the
sugar crystals and leave in a
warm place to rise for 15
minutes. Preheat the oven to
moderately hot (200°C, 400°F,
Gas Mark 6).

Bake the loaf for 25–30
minutes and allow to cool on a
wire rack.

Creamy Rice Flan

1 (212-g/7½-oz) packet frozen puff pastry
FILLING
100 g/4 oz short-grain rice
600 ml/1 pint milk
300 ml/½ pint single cream
¼ teaspoon salt
3 tablespoons castor sugar
2 eggs plus 2 egg yolks
40 g/1½ oz chopped mixed peel
50 g/2 oz red and yellow glacé cherries, chopped
25 g/1 oz almonds, chopped
50 g/2 oz raisins
icing sugar to sprinkle

Allow the pastry to thaw for 1 hour at room temperature.

Put the rice, milk, cream, salt and 2 tablespoons of the castor sugar into a saucepan and bring to the boil. Cover and simmer for 20–25 minutes, until the rice is tender and has absorbed all the liquid.
Cool then beat in the eggs and 1 egg yolk.

Preheat the oven to moderately hot (200°C, 400°F, Gas Mark 6). Roll out the pastry to line a 23-cm/9-inch flan ring and bake blind for 10 minutes. Mix all the rice with the candied peel and spread half into the pastry case. Mix the remainder with the cherries, almonds and raisins, spoon over and smooth the top. Whisk the remaining egg yolk with the castor sugar and pour over the rice mixture. Bake in the oven for a further 25 minutes. Cool then sprinkle with icing sugar.

Chelsea Cake

500 g/1 lb plain flour
40 g/1½ oz fresh yeast
60 g/2 oz castor sugar
250 ml/8 fl oz lukewarm milk
100 g/3½ oz margarine, melted
FILLING
200 g/7 oz raisins
2 tablespoons rum
125 g/4½ oz butter, melted
125 g/4½ oz granulated sugar
60 g/2 oz ground almonds
2 teaspoons ground cinnamon
80 g/3 oz chopped mixed peel
GLAZE
1 egg yolk, beaten
2 tablespoons apricot jam

Sift the flour into a bowl and make a well. Cream the yeast with a little of the sugar and the milk and pour into the well. Sprinkle over a little flour, cover and leave in a warm place for 15 minutes, until frothy. Add the margarine with the remaining sugar and mix to a dough. Knead lightly then leave to rise for 1 hour.

Soak the raisins in the rum. Knead the dough again then roll out to 3 mm/⅛ inch thick and brush with the butter. Sprinkle with the sugar, almonds, cinnamon, raisins and chopped peel. Cut the dough into 5-cm/2-inch wide strips. Roll up one strip and place in the centre of a greased 25-cm/10-inch flan tin. Roll the remaining strips around it and leave in a warm place for 15 minutes. Preheat the oven to hot (220°C, 425°F, Gas Mark 7).

Brush with beaten egg yolk and bake the cake for 35 minutes. Cool then spread with the warmed jam.

Note To make individual buns, as illustrated on the jacket, roll up the strips of dough separately and place in a cake tin. Bake and glaze as above.

181

Arabian Honey Cake

75 g/3 oz butter
3 eggs
125 g/4½ oz castor sugar
few drops of vanilla essence
2 tablespoons double cream
150 g/5 oz plain flour
½ teaspoon baking powder
TOPPING
100 g/4 oz butter
80 g/3 oz castor sugar
75 g/3 oz thick honey
2 tablespoons double cream
150 g/5 oz flaked almonds
¼ teaspoon ground cinnamon
grated rind of ½ orange

Grease a 25-cm/10-inch sandwich tin. Preheat the oven to moderately hot (200°C, 400°F, Gas Mark 6).

Melt the butter. Whisk the eggs with the sugar and vanilla essence until frothy. Stir in the cooled butter and the cream.

Sift the flour and baking powder into the mixture and fold in thoroughly. Turn into the prepared tin, smooth over and bake for 10–12 minutes.

Meanwhile, make the topping. Melt the butter in a pan and add the sugar, honey, cream, almonds, cinnamon and orange rind. Stir the ingredients well to mix and bring them to the boil. Spread this mixture over the cake and return to the oven for a further 15–20 minutes. Loosen the cake from the tin and leave to cool on a wire rack.

Iced Banana Ring

225 g/8 oz margarine or butter
150 g/5 oz castor sugar
pinch of salt
5 eggs, separated
15 g/½ oz candied ginger, chopped
75 g/3 oz desiccated coconut
grated rind of 1 lemon
500 g/1 lb bananas
3 tablespoons lemon juice
1 tablespoon rum
250 g/9 oz plain flour
1 teaspoon baking powder
ICING
200 g/7 oz icing sugar
2–3 tablespoons lemon juice

Grease a fluted 23-cm/9-inch ring tin. Preheat the oven to moderately hot (200°C, 400°F, Gas Mark 6).

Beat the margarine with the sugar and salt until light and creamy. Add the egg yolks one at a time with the ginger, coconut and lemon rind. Mix well. Peel the bananas, dice and sprinkle with the lemon juice and rum. Fold into the egg mixture. Sift the flour with the baking powder and fold in. Whisk the egg whites until very stiff and carefully fold into e mixture. Turn into the prepared tin and bake for 1–1¼ hours. Turn out and leave to cool on a wire rack.

Mix the sifted icing sugar with the lemon juice until smooth and use to ice the cake.

Cinnamon and Almond Flan

PASTRY
250 g/9 oz plain flour
125 g/4½ oz margarine, cut into
  flakes
75 g/3 oz castor sugar
1 egg
2–3 tablespoons water
pinch of salt
FILLING
3 eggs
125 ml/4 fl oz double cream
125 ml/4 fl oz milk
150 g/5 oz castor sugar
pinch of salt
1 teaspoon ground cinnamon
¼ teaspoon baking powder
200 g/7 oz ground almonds
5 plain sweet biscuits, crushed
50 g/2 oz candied lemon peel,
  finely chopped

Sift the flour into a mixing bowl and add the margarine, sugar, egg, water and salt. Mix

to a dough, wrap in foil or cling film and leave in the refrigerator for 2 hours.

Preheat the oven to moderately hot (200°C, 400°F, Gas Mark 6). Roll out the pastry on a floured surface and use to line the base and sides of a 23-cm/10-inch flan ring or springform cake tin. Bake blind for 10 minutes.

Beat the eggs with the cream, milk, sugar, salt, cinnamon and baking powder. Add the ground almonds, biscuit crumbs and chopped peel and spread this filling into the pastry case. Bake the flan for a further 45–50 minutes, then allow to cool on a wire rack.

Mizzi's Fruit Cake

100 g/4 oz prunes, stoned
50 g/2 oz dried apricots
50 g/2 oz raisins
100 g/4 oz walnuts, chopped
225 g/8 oz soft margarine
225 g/8 oz castor sugar
pinch of salt
grated rind of 1 lemon
¼ teaspoon vanilla essence
4 eggs
350 g/12 oz plain flour
1 teaspoon baking powder
icing sugar to sprinkle

Grease a 20-cm/8-inch fluted oval or round cake tin. Preheat the oven to moderate (160°C, 325°F, Gas Mark 3).

Cut the prunes and apricots into small pieces and mix them with the raisins and walnuts.

Beat the margarine with the sugar, salt, lemon rind and vanilla, until light and creamy.

Beat in the eggs one at a time, adding a tablespoon of flour with each egg after the first. Sift the remaining flour and baking powder and fold into the cake mixture. Turn into the prepared cake tin and smooth over the surface. Bake for about 1½–1¾ hours, testing with a skewer to see if cooked.

Turn the cake out on to a wire rack, allow to cool and dust with sifted icing sugar.

183

Cakes for Everyday

Mirandola Noodle Cake

500 g/1 lb plain flour
5 eggs
1 tablespoon Maraschino
4 teaspoons lukewarm water
100 g/4 oz coconut macaroons
200 g/7 oz almonds, finely chopped
300 g/11 oz castor sugar
1 tablespoon vanilla sugar
6 tablespoons milk
2 eggs

Grease a 23-cm/9-inch flan tin and dust with flour.

Sift the flour into a bowl and mix with the eggs, Maraschino and water, to form a firm pastry. Halve the dough and roll out one half until almost thin enough to see your hand through it. Leave it to dry out on an oiled surface then cut into strips approximately 1·5 mm/$\frac{1}{16}$ inch wide and 3·5 cm/$1\frac{1}{2}$ inches long.

Preheat the oven to moderately hot (200°C, 400°F, Gas Mark 6). Roll out the remaining pastry and line the prepared flan tin with it. Crumble the macaroons and mix with the almonds, sugar and vanilla sugar. Place alternate layers of the maca-roon mixture and noodles into the pastry case, finally topping with a layer of noodles. Whisk the milk and eggs together and pour over the cake. Bake for 35–40 minutes and serve warm.

Date and Fig Flan

PASTRY
200 g/7 oz plain flour
100 g/3$\frac{1}{2}$ oz butter, cut into flakes
30 g/1 oz castor sugar
1 egg yolk
pinch of salt
2 tablespoons water

FILLING
120 g/4 oz butter
200 g/7 oz castor sugar
4 eggs, separated
grated rind of 1 lemon
1 teaspoon ground cinnamon
1 teaspoon each of ground nutmeg and ground cloves
$\frac{1}{4}$ teaspoon salt
100 g/4 oz ground hazelnuts
75 g/3 oz self-raising flour
75 g/3 oz walnuts, chopped
75 g/3 oz figs, finely chopped
75 g/3 oz dates, finely chopped

Sift the flour into a bowl and add the flaked butter, sugar, egg yolk, salt and water. Mix the ingredients to form a pastry dough, cover and leave in the refrigerator for 2 hours.

Preheat the oven to moderate (180°C, 350°F, Gas Mark 4). Roll out the pastry to line a 23-cm/9-inch flan tin. Beat the butter with the sugar until light and creamy. Add the egg yolks, lemon rind, spices, salt and hazelnuts. Whisk the egg whites until stiff and fold into the egg yolk mixture. Mix the sifted flour with the walnuts, figs and dates and fold carefully into the egg mixture. Spread the filling into the pastry case and bake for 55–60 minutes. Cool on a wire rack.

Plum Lattice Tart

PASTRY
300 g / 11 oz plain flour
pinch of salt
180 g / 6 oz butter, cut into flakes
1 egg yolk
120 g / 4 oz castor sugar
FILLING
1 kg / 2 lb plums
2 tablespoons cornflour
150 g / 5 oz sugar
25 g / 1 oz butter
50 g / 2 oz walnuts, chopped
icing sugar to sprinkle

Sift the flour into a mixing bowl and add the salt, flaked butter, egg yolk and sugar. Mix to a pastry dough, cover and leave in the refrigerator for 1 hour.

Wash, stone and quarter the plums and cook in a little water for 5 minutes. Mix the cornflour with 3 tablespoons cold water and stir into the plums with the sugar. Continue to cook until thickened, stirring all the time. Remove from the heat and stir in the butter and walnuts. Leave to cool.

Preheat the oven to moderately hot (200°C, 400°F, Gas Mark 6). Roll out the pastry to line a 23-cm/9-inch flan tin, reserving enough pastry to make the lattice. Spread the plum filling into the flan case. Cut the remaining pastry into thin strips and arrange in a lattice pattern over the plums.

Bake for 35–45 minutes. Sprinkle with sifted icing sugar to serve.

Grape Cream Flan

PASTRY
300 g / 10 oz plain flour
200 g / 7 oz butter, cut into flakes
100 g / 3¼ oz castor sugar
1 egg
FILLING
600 ml / 1 pint milk
50 g / 2 oz cornflour
25 g / 1 oz castor sugar
2 eggs, separated
500 g / 1 lb black grapes, washed and pips removed
150 ml / ¼ pint double cream

Place the sifted flour in a mixing bowl with the butter, sugar and egg and mix until a dough is formed. Wrap in foil or cling film and leave in the refrigerator for 2 hours.

Preheat the oven to moderately hot (190°C, 375°F, Gas Mark 5). Roll out the pastry to line a 23-cm/9-inch flan tin and bake blind for 20 minutes, until cooked. Allow the pastry to cool.

Blend 4 tablespoons milk with the cornflour, sugar and egg yolks. Bring the remaining milk to the boil and pour on to the cornflour. Return to the heat and bring to the boil, stirring until thickened. Allow to cool, stirring frequently to prevent a skin forming. Whisk the egg whites until stiff and fold into the cooled mixture. Place half this filling in the pastry case. Reserve 12 grapes for decoration and place the remainder on top of the filling. Cover with the remaining filling, smoothing evenly. Chill in the refrigerator until set.

Decorate the flan with piped whipped cream and grapes.

Cakes for Everyday

Baked Vanilla Cheesecake

PASTRY
250 g/9 oz plain flour
125 g/4½ oz butter, cut into flakes
pinch of salt
30 g/1 oz castor sugar
1 egg
2–3 tablespoons water
FILLING
675 g/1½ lb curd or cream cheese
3 tablespoons oil
275 g/10 oz castor sugar
3 eggs, separated
3 tablespoons cornflour
few drops of vanilla essence
6 tablespoons milk

Sift the flour into a bowl. Add the butter, salt, sugar, egg and water and mix to a dough. Wrap in foil or cling film and leave for 2 hours in the refrigerator.

Preheat the oven to moderate (180°C, 350°F, Gas Mark 4). Roll out the pastry to line the base and sides of a 25-cm/10-inch flan tin. Mix the cheese with the oil, sugar, egg yolks, cornflour, vanilla essence and milk, until smooth. Whisk the egg whites until stiff and fold into the cheese mixture. Pour into the pastry case and bake in the centre of the oven for 50–60 minutes.

Rich Lemon Cheesecake

BISCUIT BASE
175 g/6 oz digestive biscuits
75 g/3 oz margarine, melted
FILLING
575 g/1¼ lb cream cheese
6 eggs, separated
100 g/4 oz castor sugar
1 (142-ml/5-fl oz) carton soured cream
grated rind of 1 lemon
1 tablespoon lemon juice
2 tablespoons cornflour
1 teaspoon baking powder

Crush the biscuits into crumbs and mix with the melted margarine. Press on to the base of a greased 25-cm/10-inch springform cake tin. Preheat the oven to moderate (160°C, 325°F, Gas Mark 3).
Beat the cream cheese with the egg yolks, sugar, soured cream, lemon rind and juice, cornflour and baking powder, mixing until smooth. Whisk the egg whites until stiff and fold into the cheese mixture. Pour into the prepared tin and bake in the centre of the oven for 1¼–1½ hours. Cover with foil if becoming too brown. The cheesecake should be firm to the touch, but still slightly springy. Loosen the sides immediately with a knife and allow to cool.

Swiss Choux Rings

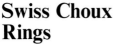

CHOUX PASTE
60 g/2 oz butter
250 ml/8 fl oz water
pinch of salt
200 g/7 oz plain flour
4 eggs
ICING
50 g/2 oz apricot jam
100 g/4 oz plain chocolate
FILLING
40 g/1½ oz cornflour
180 g/6 oz castor sugar
4 eggs, separated
500 ml/17 fl oz milk
½ teaspoon vanilla essence

Preheat the oven to hot (220°C, 425°F, Gas Mark 7). Grease a baking tray.

Heat the butter in the water until melted, add the salt and bring to the boil. Tip in the sifted flour all at once and stir vigorously until the mixture leaves the sides of the pan and forms a smooth ball. Leave to cool slightly then add the eggs one at a time. Pipe 16 small rings on to the baking tray and bake for 20 minutes. Split the rings after cooking to allow steam to escape.

Warm the jam and spread over the top of the rings. Melt the chocolate in a basin over hot water and pour over the jam on the rings.

Blend the cornflour with the sugar, egg yolks and a little of the milk. Heat the remaining milk then pour on to the blended mixture together with the vanilla essence. Return to the pan and bring to the boil, stirring continuously. Boil for a few seconds then cool slightly. Whisk the egg whites until stiff and fold into the cornflour custard which should be just warm. Cool completely, cut the rings in half and fill with the cornflour custard.

Iced Vanilla Slices

1 (368-g/13-oz) packet frozen puff pastry
ICING
200 g/7 oz icing sugar
1 tablespoon water
1 tablespoon lemon juice
FILLING
4 eggs, separated
150 g/5 oz icing sugar
50 g/2 oz cornflour
30 g/1 oz castor sugar
½ teaspoon vanilla essence
500 ml/17 fl oz milk

Allow the pastry to thaw for 1 hour at room temperature. Preheat the oven to hot (220°C, 425°F, Gas Mark 7).

Roll out the pastry to an oblong 60 × 45 cm/24 × 18 inches. Cut it in half widthways and place on a baking tray sprinkled with cold water. Prick with a fork and leave to stand in a cool place for 15 minutes. Bake the pastry for 12–18 minutes then leave to cool on a wire rack.

Mix the sifted icing sugar with the water and lemon juice and ice one of the pastry pieces.

Prepare the filling. Whisk the egg whites with the sifted icing sugar until stiff and glossy. Blend the cornflour with the egg yolks, castor sugar, vanilla essence and a little milk. Bring the remaining milk to the boil and pour on to the cornflour mixture. Return to the heat and cook for a few minutes, stirring until thickened. Fold in the whisked egg whites and leave to cool. Spread this filling thickly over the piece of pastry without icing and put the iced pastry on top.

Leave in the refrigerator until set and then cut into slices.

Toasted Aniseed Cake

5 eggs, separated
125 g/5 oz castor sugar
3 tablespoons water
175 g/6 oz plain flour
1 tablespoon ground aniseed

Grease two 0·5-kg/1-lb loaf tins. Preheat the oven to moderate (180°C, 350°F, Gas Mark 4).

Whisk the egg yolks with the sugar and water until pale and creamy. Sift the flour and add it to the yolk mixture with the aniseed. Whisk the egg whites until stiff and fold in. Divide the cake mixture between the two tins and smooth over. Bake for 40–45 minutes.

Turn the cakes out on to wire racks to cool and leave for 2 days. Preheat the oven to moderately hot (200°C, 400°F, Gas Mark 6). Cut the cakes into 1-cm/½-inch thick slices, and arrange on baking trays. Brown in the oven for 5 minutes on each side. Alternatively, toast the slices under a hot grill.

Cook's Tip
This toasted aniseed cake tastes best spread with butter and honey.

Hazelnut Buns

500 g/1 lb plain flour
30 g/1 oz fresh yeast
250 ml/8 fl oz lukewarm milk
60 g/2 oz sugar
60 g/2 oz butter, melted
1 egg
pinch of salt
grated rind of 1 lemon
1 egg yolk, beaten to glaze
FILLING
200 g/7 oz ground hazelnuts
100 g/3¼ oz castor sugar
2 tablespoons rum
2 egg whites

Sift the flour into a bowl and make a well in the centre. Cream the yeast with a little of the milk, add the remaining milk and the sugar and pour into the well in the flour. Cover and leave in a warm place for 15 minutes, until frothy. Add the butter, egg, salt and lemon rind to the yeast mixture and mix thoroughly with the flour.

Knead the dough until smooth and elastic, then leave to rise in a warm place for 15 minutes.

To make the filling, mix the hazelnuts, sugar, rum and egg whites together. Roll out the dough until it is 3–5 mm/⅛–¼ inch thick, and cut out 24 rounds, each 7·5 cm/3 inches in diameter. Divide the filling between half the rounds, leaving the edges free. Brush the edges with beaten egg yolk and cover with the remaining rounds. Press the edges together well to seal and brush the buns with beaten egg yolk. Cut a cross on the top of each bun and place on greased baking trays. Leave to rise for a further 15 minutes.

Preheat the oven to hot (220°C, 425°F, Gas Mark 7) and bake the buns for 15 minutes.

Great Traditional Cakes

Chocolate Gâteau Alice

140 g/5 oz plain chocolate
140 g/5 oz butter, softened
160 g/6 oz castor sugar
3 eggs, separated
80 g/3 oz ground almonds
80 g/3 oz rye or wheat flour
ICING
100 g/4 oz almond paste
100 g/4 oz plain chocolate
12 almonds
sugar crystals

Grease a 20-cm/8-inch spring-form cake tin and sprinkle with breadcrumbs. Preheat the oven to moderate (180°C, 350°F, Gas Mark 4).

Melt the chocolate in a basin over hot water. Cream the butter with half the sugar until light and fluffy. Stir in the melted chocolate, egg yolks and ground almonds. Whisk the egg whites until stiff and fold in the remaining sugar. Fold into the chocolate mixture and finally fold in the flour. Turn into the prepared tin and bake for 40–45 minutes.

Roll out the almond paste thinly and use to cover the top and sides of the cake. Melt the chocolate in a basin over hot water and coat the cake thinly using a palette knife. Dip the tip of the almonds in a little melted chocolate, turn them in the sugar crystals and decorate the cake as illustrated.

Sachertorte

SPONGE MIXTURE
7 eggs, separated
200 g/7 oz castor sugar
50 g/2 oz cocoa powder
100 g/4 oz plain flour
100 g/4 oz butter, melted
50 g/2 oz biscuit crumbs
ICING
5 tablespoons apricot jam
225 g/8 oz plain chocolate
6 tablespoons double cream
175 g/6 oz icing sugar
chocolate vermicelli to sprinkle

Grease two 23-cm/9-inch sandwich tins and sprinkle with dry breadcrumbs. Preheat the oven to moderately hot (200°C, 400°F, Gas Mark 6).

Whisk the egg yolks with 100 g/4 oz castor sugar until thick and light. Fold in the sifted cocoa powder and flour with the cooled, melted butter. Whisk the egg whites until frothy. Add the remaining castor sugar and whisk until stiff. Fold into the egg yolk mixture with the biscuit crumbs.

Spoon the mixture into the prepared tins and bake in the centre of the oven for 30 minutes. Reduce the heat to moderate (180°C, 350°F, Gas Mark 4) and bake for a further 15–20 minutes. Cool in the oven, with the door slightly open, for 15 minutes, then remove to cool completely.

Warm the jam and use to sandwich the layers and spread thinly over the top and sides of the cake. Melt the chocolate in a basin over hot water. Cool, then beat in the cream and sifted icing sugar. Spread this icing smoothly over the cake and sprinkle a little chocolate vermicelli around the base of the cake, if liked.

Viennese Chocolate Cake

CAKE MIXTURE
6 eggs, separated
1 tablespoon vanilla sugar
pinch of salt
150 g/5 oz castor sugar
100 g/3¼ oz plain chocolate, grated
100 g/3¼ oz biscuit crumbs
100 g/3½ oz ground hazelnuts
FILLING
3 tablespoons sherry
300 g/11 oz apricot jam
ICING
120 g/4 oz plain chocolate
1 egg
200 g/7 oz icing sugar
60 g/2 oz butter

Grease the base of a 25-cm/10-inch springform cake tin. Preheat the oven to moderate (180°C, 350°F, Gas Mark 4).

Whisk the egg yolks, vanilla sugar, salt and sugar together until pale and creamy. Stir in the grated chocolate. Whisk the egg whites until stiff and fold carefully into the yolk mixture. Mix the biscuit crumbs with the hazelnuts and fold in. Turn the mixture into the cake tin, smooth the surface and bake for 50–60 minutes. Turn the cake out on to a wire rack and leave to cool.

Cut the cake through twice to make three layers and soak each layer with sherry. Soften the jam and use to sandwich the layers together.

Melt the chocolate in a basin over a pan of hot water and allow to cool a little. Stir in the egg and sifted icing sugar. Melt the butter and add this to the chocolate, beating well until the mixture is creamy. Cover the top and sides of the cake with this and use a palette knife to swirl the icing. Allow the icing to set before cutting the cake.

Cook's Tip

This cake may also be filled with almond paste. Knead 225 g/8 oz almond paste, divide it in half and roll out each half into a thin round the size of the cake. Sandwich the cake layers together with the almond paste and apricot jam then ice as in the recipe.

Brandy Snap Ring

CAKE MIXTURE
175 g/6 oz butter
175 g/6 oz castor sugar
¼ teaspoon salt
3 eggs
1 tablespoon rum
grated rind and juice of ½ lemon
150 g/5 oz plain flour
1 tablespoon baking powder
75 g/3 oz cornflour
ICING
175 g/6 oz butter
350 g/12 oz icing sugar
1 egg yolk
6–8 brandy snaps, crushed
150 ml/¼ pint double cream
8 glacé cherries

Grease a 23-cm/9-inch ring tin. Preheat the oven to moderate (180°C, 350°F, Gas Mark 4).

Cream the butter with the castor sugar until light and fluffy. Beat in the salt, eggs, rum, lemon rind and juice. Fold in the sifted flour, baking powder and cornflour. Pour into the ring tin and bake for 45–60 minutes. Cool slightly in the tin, then turn out on to a wire rack to cool completely. Cut into four layers.

Cream the butter with the sifted icing sugar and egg yolk. Use to sandwich together the four layers and to cover the whole cake. Press on the crushed brandy snaps to cover completely. Decorate with the cream, whipped and piped, and halved glacé cherries.

Chocolate Délice

100 g/4 oz butter
100 g/4 oz castor sugar
100 g/4 oz plain chocolate
6 eggs, separated
100 g/4 oz ground almonds
50 g/2 oz biscuit crumbs
75 g/3 oz plain flour
DECORATION AND ICING
50 g/2 oz slivered almonds
100 g/4 oz plain chocolate

Grease a 30-cm/12-inch long Balmoral cake tin or 1-kg/2-lb loaf tin and dust with flour. Preheat the oven to moderate (180°C, 350°F, Gas Mark 4).

Beat the butter and sugar together until pale and creamy. Break the chocolate into small pieces and melt in a basin over hot water. Add it to the butter mixture together with the egg yolks. Beat the mixture thoroughly until very creamy. Stir in the ground almonds, biscuit crumbs and sifted flour.

Whisk the egg whites until stiff and fold into the cake mixture. Turn into the prepared tin and bake the cake for 50–60 minutes. Turn the cake out on to a wire rack to cool and press the almonds into it as illustrated. Melt the chocolate in a basin over hot water and cover the cake thickly with this icing.

Raspberry and Lemon Cream Gâteau

1 (20-cm/8-inch) chocolate
  cake (see page 228)
FILLING AND TOPPING
600 ml/1 pint double cream
100 g/4 oz icing sugar
grated rind and juice of 1 lemon
225 g/8 oz fresh or frozen
  raspberries
1 tablespoon Maraschino
25 g/1 oz macaroons, crushed
16 thin slices lemon

Make the chocolate cake (see page 228) and cut horizontally into three layers.

Whip the cream with the sifted icing sugar until stiff and divide into three portions. Mix one portion with the lemon rind and juice. Reserve 16 raspberries, purée the remainder and mix with the second portion of cream. Put each of the two flavoured creams into a separate piping bag and pipe alternate rings of raspberry cream and lemon cream over two of the cake layers, until the layers are completely covered. Sandwich the layers together and place the third cake layer on top.

Mix the final portion of cream with the liqueur and spread it over the top and sides of the gâteau, reserving a little for piping. Mark the top of the gâteau into 16 slices with a knife. Sprinkle the centre and base of the cake with crushed macaroons and decorate each slice with a rosette of cream, a slice of lemon and a raspberry. Serve immediately.

Cook's Tip

If the cake is not to be served immediately, open freeze without the decoration. Decorate when thawed and ready to serve.

Charlotte Royal

SWISS ROLL MIXTURE
4 eggs, separated, plus 2 egg
  yolks
100 g/4 oz castor sugar
pinch of salt
few drops of vanilla essence
75 g/3 oz plain flour
25 g/1 oz cornflour
450 g/1 lb cherry or raspberry
  jam
FILLING
15 g/½ oz powdered gelatine
250 ml/8 fl oz white wine
100 g/4 oz sugar
1 tablespoon lemon juice
pinch of salt
350 ml/12 fl oz double cream
glacé cherries to decorate

Make the Swiss roll (see page 228), adding the salt and vanilla essence to the whisked egg mixture. Turn out on to sugared paper, strip off the lining paper and spread all over with the jam while still

warm. Trim the edges and roll up tightly, using the sugared paper to help you. Leave to cool.

Cut the Swiss roll into 18 slices. Line a 1·5-litre/2½-pint pudding basin with 14 of the slices, pressing well against each other to cover the base and sides.

Dissolve the gelatine in 4 tablespoons wine over a gentle heat. Heat the remaining wine with the sugar, lemon juice and salt, then pour on to the dissolved gelatine and stir to mix. Allow to cool until just on the point of setting. Whip the cream and reserve a little for piping. Pour the wine mixture into the cream and fold together carefully. Place in the lined basin and cover with the remaining Swiss roll slices. Chill in the refrigerator until set.

Turn out on to a serving plate and decorate with rosettes of cream and glacé cherries.

Bilberry Cream Torte

PASTRY
160 g/6 oz plain flour
80 g/3 oz butter, cut into flakes
40 g/1½ oz castor sugar
pinch of salt
1 egg yolk
1–2 tablespoons water
TOPPING
500 g/1 lb bilberries
1–2 tablespoons orange liqueur
15 g/½ oz powdered gelatine
450 ml/¾ pint double cream
50 g/2 oz icing sugar
1 small packet quick-setting
  jel mix
100 g/4 oz toasted flaked
  almonds

Place the sifted flour in a mixing bowl and add the butter, sugar, salt, egg yolk and water. Mix quickly to a dough, cover and leave in the refrigerator for 1 hour.

Wash the bilberries, dry them and steep in the liqueur for 30 minutes.

Preheat the oven to hot (220°C, 425°F, Gas Mark 7). Roll out the pastry to cover the base of a 20–23-cm/8–9-inch springform cake tin. Prick the base and bake for about 15 minutes, until cooked. Leave to cool on a wire rack.

Dissolve the gelatine in 3 tablespoons water over a gentle heat. Whip the cream with the sifted icing sugar until stiff and fold in the cooled gelatine and three-quarters of the bilberries. Place on top of the cooked pastry and smooth over evenly. Cover with the remaining bilberries. Make up the jel mix according to the packet instructions, and pour over the fruit. Leave in the refrigerator until set.

Remove the cake from the tin and sprinkle the sides generously with flaked almonds.

203

Black Forest Cherry Gâteau

CAKE MIXTURE
100 g/4 oz plain chocolate
100 g/4 oz butter
100 g/4 oz castor sugar
4 eggs
75 g/3 oz ground almonds
50 g/2 oz plain flour
50 g/2 oz cornflour
2 teaspoons baking powder
FILLING AND TOPPING
450 ml/¾ pint double cream
2 (425-g/15-oz) cans pitted
  cherries, drained
6 tablespoons Kirsch
12 glacé cherries
chocolate caraque (see page 231)

Lightly grease three 18-cm/7-inch sandwich tins. Preheat the oven to moderate (180°C, 350°F, Gas Mark 4).

Melt the chocolate in a basin over a pan of hot water. Cool. Cream the butter and sugar until light and fluffy. Beat in the eggs, almonds and melted chocolate. Sift the flour, cornflour and baking powder on to the creamed mixture and fold in, mixing well. Turn into the sandwich tins and bake for 20–25 minutes, until cooked. Leave to cool in the tin for a few minutes before turning out on to a wire rack.

Whip the cream until thick. Dry the cherries on absorbent paper. Sprinkle each cooled cake layer with 2 tablespoons Kirsch. Sandwich together with the cherries and cream, leaving enough cream to spread over the top and sides of the cake, and to pipe a border. Decorate with the glacé cherries and pile chocolate caraque in the centre.

Chess Board Chocolate Cake

1 (20-cm/8-inch) chocolate
  cake (see page 228)
3 tablespoons orange liqueur
FILLING AND TOPPING
6 tablespoons milk
450 g/1 lb curd or cream cheese
150 g/5 oz castor sugar
grated rind and juice of 1
  orange and 1 lemon
20 g/¾ oz powdered gelatine
450 ml/¾ pint double cream
DECORATION
16 small pieces orange
8 glacé cherries, halved
2 teaspoons chopped pistachio
  nuts
chocolate vermicelli

Make the chocolate cake (see page 228), cool and cut horizontally into three layers. Sprinkle each layer with liqueur. Cut two layers into 2·5-cm/1-inch wide rings, working from the outside inwards, and leave one layer whole to use as a base.

Beat the milk, cheese, sugar, fruit rinds and juice until smooth. Dissolve the gelatine in 3 tablespoons water over a gentle heat and stir into the cheese mixture. Whip the cream until stiff and fold it into the cheese mixture. Spread very thinly over the cake base. Using the first cut out layer place the largest ring (to fit the outside of the cake) on the base and then the alternate cake rings. Fill the gaps in between with the cream, smoothing evenly. Then place the remaining rings alternately on top to form the next layer. Fill these gaps with more cream. Repeat this procedure using the second cake layer, to form a chess board pattern. Finally cover the whole cake with the cream, pipe 16 rosettes on top and decorate as illustrated.

Great Traditional Cakes

Raspberry Cream Torte

SHORTBREAD BASE
100 g/3¼ oz butter or margarine
50 g/2 oz castor sugar
150 g/5 oz plain flour
SPONGE MIXTURE
*4 eggs, separated, plus 2 egg
    yolks*
100 g/4 oz castor sugar
80 g/3 oz plain flour
25 g/1 oz cornflour
35 g/1½ oz cocoa powder
FILLING
*450 g/1 lb fresh or frozen
    raspberries*
*1 tablespoon raspberry liqueur
    or Kirsch*
15 g/½ oz powdered gelatine
450 ml/¾ pint double cream
70 g/2¼ oz icing sugar
DECORATION
250 ml/8 fl oz double cream
1 tablespoon icing sugar
*25 g/1 oz toasted flaked
    almonds*

Cream the butter with the
sugar. Add the sifted flour and
work into a dough. Wrap in
foil or cling film and leave in
the refrigerator for 2 hours.

If using frozen raspberries,
allow to defrost at room
temperature.

Grease a 23 × 33-cm/9 ×
13-inch Swiss roll tin and line
with greased greaseproof paper.
Preheat the oven to hot (220°C,
425°F, Gas Mark 7). Whisk all
the egg yolks with half the
sugar until thick and creamy.
Whisk the whites until stiff
then whisk in the remaining
sugar and fold into the egg
yolk mixture. Sift the flour,
cornflour and cocoa powder
on to the eggs and fold in
carefully using a metal spoon.
Spread this mixture into the
prepared tin and bake for
10–12 minutes. Turn the
sponge out on to clean greaseproof paper sprinkled with
sugar. Remove the lining
paper from the cake, cover

with a damp cloth and leave
to cool.

Reduce the oven temperature
to moderately hot (190°C,
375°F, Gas Mark 5). Roll out
the shortbread dough to line
the base of a 20-cm/8-inch
springform cake tin. Bake for
15–20 minutes and leave to
cool in the tin.

Lightly crush two-thirds of
the raspberries and mix with
the liqueur. Reserve the
remaining fruit for decoration.
Dissolve the gelatine in 3
tablespoons cold water over a
gentle heat. Whip the cream
with the sifted icing sugar until
stiff. Fold in the cooled gelatine together with the raspberries. Spread the sponge
evenly with the fruit and
cream mixture and cut lengthways into 5·5-cm/2¼-inch
strips. Roll up one of the
strips and stand upright on the
centre of the shortbread. Shape
the other strips carefully into
circles around the central roll,

until the whole base has been
covered. Place the cake in the
refrigerator and leave to set.

Whip the cream for decoration with the sifted icing sugar
until stiff. Remove the cake
from the tin and place on a
serving plate. Spread some of
the whipped cream over the
top and sides of the cake,
smoothing with a palette knife.
Place the remainder in a piping
bag and pipe an attractive
design on top of the cake, as
illustrated. Decorate the
rosettes with the reserved
raspberries and sprinkle flaked
almonds over the centre.

Cherry Cream Layer Gâteau

1 (368-g/13-oz) packet frozen
  puff pastry
FILLING AND TOPPING
50 g/2 oz redcurrant jelly
100 g/4 oz icing sugar
1 tablespoon lemon juice
1 (425-g/15-oz) can red
  cherries
pinch of ground cinnamon
1 tablespoon cornflour
450 ml/¾ pint double cream
40 g/1½ oz castor sugar
12 glacé cherries

Allow the pastry to thaw for 1
hour at room temperature.
Sprinkle a baking tray with
cold water. Preheat the oven to
moderately hot (200°C, 400°F,
Gas Mark 6).

Divide the pastry into three
portions and roll out each into
a 20-cm/8-inch round. Arrange
on the baking tray and leave
for 15 minutes. Bake for 10–12
minutes, until lightly browned.

Cover the best pastry round
with the warmed redcurrant
jelly. Mix the sifted icing sugar
and lemon juice together and
spread this glaze over the jam.
Leave to cool then divide the
glazed pastry layer into 12
slices.

Drain the cherries, reserving
the juice. Heat the juice from
the cherries with the cinnamon.
Blend the cornflour with a
little cold water and add to the
cherry juice. Bring to the boil,
stirring continuously until
slightly thickened. Stir in the
stoned cherries and leave to

cool. Spread the cooled cherry
sauce over the bottom pastry
layer.

Whip the cream with the
castor sugar until stiff. Put
about 5 tablespoons of this
cream into a piping bag fitted
with a star nozzle. Spread
some of the remaining cream
over the cherries and put the
last uncovered pastry layer on
top. Spread the remaining
cream thickly over this and
around the sides of the gâteau.
Arrange the glazed pastry
slices on top and decorate
each with a rosette of cream
and glacé cherry.

Cook's Tip

It is important to cut the
glazed pastry layer into
slices before placing over
the cream filling. If you
try to cut it when serving
the gâteau, the cream
filling will spill out.

Chocolate Hazelnut Meringue

6 egg whites
200 g/7 oz castor sugar
80 g/3 oz icing sugar
1 tablespoon cornflour
80 g/3 oz ground hazelnuts
DECORATION AND FILLING
100 g/4 oz plain chocolate
300 ml/½ pint double cream
1 tablespoon icing sugar
1 teaspoon drinking chocolate
* powder*

Line two or three baking trays with non-stick baking parchment and draw five 23-cm/9-inch circles on them in pencil. Preheat the oven to very cool (120°C, 250°F, Gas Mark ½).

Whisk the egg whites until stiff. Add the castor sugar and whisk again until stiff. Sift the icing sugar with the corn-flour, mix with the hazelnuts and fold into the egg whites.

Spread one-fifth on each circle and dry out in the oven for 3–4 hours, leaving the oven door slightly open.

Melt the chocolate and spread thinly over waxed paper to cover an area of 24 × 30 cm/ 9 × 12 inches. Cool, then divide the largest side into ten equal strips. Cut eight of these strips equally into three, making 24 short strips of chocolate. Cut the remaining two long strips into four each, giving eight shorter strips.

Whip the cream with the sugar until stiff. Spread the meringue layers with cream and place one on top of the other. Cover the cake with the remaining cream, piping rosettes to decorate. Sift the chocolate powder over the cream, and arrange the shorter strips of chocolate on the cake, and the 24 longer strips over-lapping around the sides.

Peach Gâteau Genevieve

1 (20-cm/8-inch) chocolate
* cake (see page 228)*
FILLING AND DECORATION
450 ml/¾ pint double cream
60 g/2 oz icing sugar, sifted
30 g/1 oz cocoa powder, sifted
1 (213-g/7½-oz) can peach
* slices*
2 tablespoons Maraschino
1 tablespoon chopped pistachios
ICING
200 g/7 oz plain chocolate
100 g/4 oz icing sugar, sifted
15 g/½ oz butter

Make up the cake as on page 228 and cut into three layers.

Whip the cream with half the sugar until thick and divide into three. Mix one-third with the remaining sugar and the cocoa powder, and spread over the cake base. Halve the peach slices and place almost all over the second cake layer. Mix the second portion of cream with the liqueur and spread over the peaches. Top with the third cake layer.

Melt the chocolate and mix with the icing sugar, 2 table-spoons water and the butter. Spread smoothly over the entire cake. When cooled decorate with swirls of piped cream, peach segments and pistachios.

Note To make the variation illustrated on the jacket, use two rounds of chocolate sponge cake and one of plain. Place diced peaches and strawberries over the base and sandwich the layers with sweetened whipped cream. Spread cream all over and cover with finely grated chocolate. Decorate as illustrated.

207

Dobostorte

6 sponge rounds (see below)
FILLING
300 ml/½ pint milk
25 g/1 oz cornflour
50 g/2 oz castor sugar
1 egg yolk
250 g/9 oz butter
50 g/2 oz marshmallows
50 g/2 oz plain chocolate
CARAMEL GLAZE
200 g/7 oz sugar
15 g/½ oz butter

Prepare and bake the sponge cake layers as in the recipe for Prince Regent Cake (see right). When cool fill with the following cream mixture.

Mix a little of the milk with the cornflour. Heat the remaining milk with the sugar and pour on to the blended cornflour. Return to the heat and bring to the boil, stirring constantly until thickened. Add the egg yolk and cool.

Cream the butter until soft and then beat it, a spoonful at a time, into the cooled cornflour mixture. Melt the marshmallows and chocolate in a basin over hot water. Beat into the cooled mixture and chill until firm enough to spread.

Spread five sponge rounds with this cream and arrange on top of each other. Spread the rest of the cream around the sides of the cake.

Caramelise the sugar and butter to a light brown colour, stirring all the time. Spread this over the top of the cake immediately. While the caramel covering is still soft, divide the top into 12 slices with an oiled knife. (The caramel will certainly not cut after it has hardened.)

Prince Regent Cake

SPONGE MIXTURE
7 eggs, separated
150 g/5 oz castor sugar
pinch of salt
150 g/5 oz self-raising flour
FILLING
300 ml/½ pint milk
25 g/1 oz cornflour
50 g/2 oz castor sugar
1 egg yolk
250 g/9 oz butter
50 g/2 oz plain chocolate
50 g/2 oz cocoa powder
ICING
200 g/7 oz plain chocolate

Grease and flour three baking trays. Preheat the oven to hot (220°C, 425°F, Gas Mark 7).

Whisk the egg yolks with half the sugar and the salt until thick. Whisk the egg whites until stiff, whisk in the remaining sugar and fold into the yolks. Sift over the flour and fold in. Spread the sponge mixture into six 25-cm/10-inch rounds on the baking trays and bake in the centre of the oven for 5–7 minutes. Cool on wire racks.

Mix a little milk with the cornflour. Heat the remaining milk with the sugar and pour on to the cornflour. Return to the heat and bring to the boil, stirring. Add the egg yolk and allow to cool. Cream the butter until soft and then beat it a spoonful at a time into the cooled cornflour sauce.

Melt the chocolate in a basin over hot water and add it to the butter cream with the sifted cocoa powder. Spread over the rounds, placing one on top of the other, and use to cover the top and sides of the cake. Leave in the refrigerator until the cream has set.

Melt the chocolate for the icing and pour over the cake, smoothing with a palette knife.

Milanese Almond Cake

SPONGE MIXTURE
4 eggs
100 g/4 oz castor sugar
grated rind of ½ lemon
50 g/2 oz plain flour
25 g/1 oz cornflour
25 g/1 oz ground almonds
25 g/1 oz butter, melted
FILLING AND TOPPING
225 g/8 oz raspberry jam
400 g/14 oz ground almonds
100 g/4 oz castor sugar
6 egg yolks
4–5 tablespoons rum
1 egg white
*80 g/3 oz toasted flaked
  almonds*

Grease and flour a 20-cm/8-inch springform cake tin. Preheat the oven to moderately hot (190°C, 375°F, Gas Mark 5).
Whisk the eggs and sugar with the lemon rind until thick and creamy. Sift the flour and cornflour together, mix with the ground almonds and fold into the egg mixture using a metal spoon. Lastly fold in the melted butter. Turn into the cake tin and bake for 35–45 minutes.
Leave the cake on a wire rack to cool overnight then slice through into three layers. Sandwich the layers together with some of the raspberry jam.
Mix the ground almonds with the sugar, egg yolks and rum, until soft enough to pipe. Put half this mixture into a piping bag and mix the remainder with sufficient egg white to give a spreading consistency. Spread over the top and sides of the cake and

pipe the remainder over the cake in an attractive petal design, as illustrated, to make a flower pattern.
Preheat the oven to very hot (240°C, 475°F, Gas Mark 9) and bake the cake for a few minutes until the almond icing begins to turn light brown. Warm the remaining jam, sieve it and spread a little into the flower petals. Spread the rest of the jam over the sides of the cake and press on the toasted flaked almonds.

Cook's Tip

As the sponge is already cooked, the cake need only be put in the oven for long enough to brown and slightly crispen the top. Alternatively the cake could be placed briefly under a hot grill.

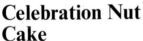

Celebration Nut Cake

SPONGE MIXTURE
5 eggs, separated
100 g/4 oz castor sugar
100 g/4 oz ground hazelnuts
2 tablespoons plain flour
¼ teaspoon almond essence
FILLING
15 g/½ oz cornflour
25 g/1 oz castor sugar
150 ml/¼ pint milk
2 egg yolks, beaten
TOPPING AND DECORATION
200 g/7 oz almond paste
100 g/4 oz icing sugar
2–3 tablespoons lemon juice
walnut halves to decorate

Grease a 20-cm/8-inch spring-form cake tin. Preheat the oven to moderately hot (190°C, 375°F, Gas Mark 5).

Whisk the egg yolks and sugar until pale and creamy and fold in the hazelnuts, sifted flour and almond essence. Whisk the egg whites until stiff and fold into the mixture. Bake the cake for 40 minutes then cool over-night on a wire rack.

Cut the cake through into two layers. Mix the cornflour with the sugar, a little of the milk and the beaten egg yolks. Bring the remaining milk to the boil. Pour on to the cornflour mixture, bring back to the boil and cook for a few seconds, stirring until thickened. Leave to cool then sandwich the cake layers together with this filling.

Knead the almond paste and roll it into a round the size of the cake. Place on the cake, pressing it in lightly. Mix the sifted icing sugar with the lemon juice and ice the cake all over. Decorate with walnut halves.

Chocolate Chestnut Gâteau

1 (20-cm/8-inch) chocolate cake (see page 228)
FILLING
1 (250-g/8¾-oz) can sweetened chestnut purée
1 tablespoon lemon juice
4 tablespoons single cream
ICING
3 tablespoons apricot jam
225 g/8 oz almond paste
175 g/6 oz plain chocolate

Make the chocolate cake (see page 228), cool and cut horizontally into three layers.

Mix the chestnut purée, lemon juice and cream together to make a smooth filling. Sandwich the layers together with this filling. Warm the jam, sieve it and brush the cake all over.

Roll out the almond paste, reserving enough to make the figures for decoration. Cover the top and sides of the cake with a thin layer of almond paste and trim the edges. Shape the reserved almond paste into small figures, as illustrated.

Melt the chocolate in a basin over hot water and cover the cake completely with this icing, smoothing it evenly with a palette knife. Decorate with the marzipan figures and allow the icing to set.

The Art of Baking

Baking is an art – but one which everyone can master with patience, a pride in working precisely and a certain amount of basic knowledge. By reading the following pages carefully, you will be able to acquire at least the beginning of this art.

Baking Hints

- Before you begin baking always remember to get out all the necessary equipment. Do not forget the small things such as spoons, knives, pastry brush, wooden spoon, pastry scraper, grater and absorbent paper, so that they are all easily available when you need them.
- Baking is an exact art! Therefore weigh or measure all necessary ingredients exactly. Unless specified otherwise, the recipes in this book have been tested using a size 3 egg: if you use smaller or larger eggs you may need to adjust the recipe accordingly.
- In our recipes we always use sifted flours. If you sift your flour you can be sure that no lumps will spoil the baking results.
- If the recipe indicates that the dough should be kneaded on a floured board, or rolled or worked in some other way, sprinkle the board with only a very little flour; dough absorbs flour readily and too much would alter the recipe proportions.
- Lemons or oranges whose rind is to be grated must be washed thoroughly beforehand.
- If the tin or baking tray is to be greased, sprinkled with breadcrumbs or flour, or lined with greaseproof paper, do this first. Then when the mixture is ready there will be no delay before baking. This is especially important with cake mixtures.
- Remember to always preheat the oven sufficient time in advance; an electric oven must be preheated 20 minutes in advance, a gas oven about 15 minutes. Place the oven shelves in the correct position before switching the oven on. As a general rule, yeast mixtures and pastry dishes should be cooked towards the top of the oven, cakes and biscuits should always be placed in the centre of the oven, while meringues should be cooked as low down in the oven as possible to prevent browning during the slow cooking time. This does not apply in fan-assisted ovens where there is constant all-round heat.
- Always place cake tins directly on to the oven shelf, never on to a baking tray, unless stipulated in the recipe.
- If the cakes are browning too quickly during baking, cover the tops with greaseproof paper or foil.
- Never open the oven door during the early cooking stage. You can look at small biscuits or cookies after 5 minutes, but generally the door should not be opened during the first 15–20 minutes.
- Test cakes with a skewer at the end of the given baking time, to see if cooked throughout. Insert a warmed metal skewer into the centre: if it comes out with no uncooked mixture clinging to it the cake is ready.

Cook's Tips

- Apples, pears and bananas quickly turn brown when peeled and cut. Always use a stainless steel knife to cut and immediately sprinkle with lemon juice or lemon juice and water.
- If pastry dough is difficult to roll place between two floured sheets of greaseproof paper, or wrap in cling film and leave to chill in the refrigerator for 30 minutes before rolling.
- If you have made up pastry that you do not wish to bake immediately, wrap it firmly in foil or cling film and place in the refrigerator. It can remain there for up to a week and then be rolled, shaped and baked.
- Fruit cake with a high dried fruit content will stay fresh and moist after cutting if you keep it well wrapped in an airtight container.
- Ground spices will not keep their flavour for much longer than a year and then only if stored in airtight and light-proof containers. It is best to buy spices unground and to mark the purchase date on the container.
- Non-stick baking parchment saves time and effort. For all kinds of biscuits line the baking tray with this paper, then the baking tray need not be greased and will remain clean. When cool it is easy to remove the biscuits from the paper with a palette knife and they will be less likely to break. The paper can be used again several times.
- It is easier to turn a cake out of the tin on to a wire cooling rack if you place the rack on the tin, hold the tin and rack with a cloth and turn both together.
- Cheesecakes and cream cheese cakes should be left to cool in the oven after baking. Turn off the oven and leave the door open until the temperature inside the oven is the same as that outside. This will prevent the cheesecake from sinking.
- You can collect egg whites for meringues. When you need an egg yolk alone for a cake or glaze, lightly whisk the white and place it in a small screw-topped jar or freezing container and then freeze it. When thawed it can be used like fresh egg white.
- When cutting out shortcrust pastry or biscuit dough with small cutters, dip the cutter into flour to make it easier.
- When baking biscuits it is a good idea to bake one or two trial biscuits to see how much they spread during baking. You can then optimise the use of the space on the baking tray.
- If you notice too late that you have no icing sugar to sift over a cake, grind granulated sugar in a coffee grinder or blender and use this instead.
- Above all familiarise yourself with the basic recipes that follow. There all the stages of work are clearly explained and much useful advice is given.

The Art of Baking

Yeast Cookery

Handling Yeast Correctly

Yeast is a living matter composed of tiny cells which, when combined with a liquid and possibly sugar at a suitable temperature, will divide continually. This produces carbon dioxide which forms bubbles in the dough, causing it to rise and give the bread its structure. Fresh yeast must be really fresh and not dried out; it should be pliable and soft to the touch, creamy in colour and crumbly when broken. Old yeast is hard, cracked and discoloured in places; in this condition it will have lost most of its effectiveness. To keep yeast fresh, store in a container with a tight-fitting lid, or wrap in cling film. It will keep for 4–5 days in a cool larder or 1–2 weeks in the refrigerator. You can also freeze fresh yeast and store it for up to 6 months in the freezer. It is advisable to divide the yeast into workable quantities e.g. 15 g/½ oz pieces, and then wrap individually in foil or freezer film.

Active dried baking yeast is composed of granules similar in colour to fresh yeast. When using dried yeast remember it is more concentrated than fresh and therefore you will need only half the stated amount of fresh yeast. Always read the instructions on the package before beginning.

Yeast works most effectively in a warm temperature and should always be allowed to reach room temperature before use. Make sure all baking ingredients are at room temperature in advance; ingredients such as milk or fat which has to be melted before adding to the dough, should never exceed 38–43°C/100–110°F. Many recipes state 'leave the dough to rise in a warm place'; the room temperature of most modern kitchens is warm enough for the yeast to act. However, the dough should always be covered with a damp cloth or cling film, to protect it from possible draughts which could prevent its rising, and also to prevent a skin forming.

Basic Yeast Dough

The following method is basically valid for all types of yeast dough. Sometimes a little sugar is added as well.

500 g/1 lb plain flour	*50 g/2 oz butter, melted*
30 g/1 oz fresh yeast	*½ teaspoon salt*
250 ml/8 fl oz lukewarm liquid	*1 egg*
(milk or water)	*1 egg yolk, beaten to glaze*

Make sure all the ingredients are at room temperature before beginning. Prepare all the necessary ingredients and equipment. Weigh solid ingredients exactly. Measure liquids precisely and bring them to the correct temperature. Grease a 1-kg/2-lb loaf tin or two 0.5-kg/1-lb loaf tins.

Sift the flour into a mixing bowl and make a well in the centre. Cream the yeast with a little of the lukewarm liquid, then add the remaining liquid. Pour into the well in the centre of the flour and sprinkle a little of the flour over the top. Cover the bowl with a damp cloth so that the warmth can circulate beneath it, and leave the mixture in a draught-free place for about 15 minutes, until the layer of flour which covers the yeast shows deep crevices and bubbles appear. It is better to rely on your eyes rather than the clock when judging whether the yeast has stood for long enough.

When ready, beat the yeast mixture into the remaining flour with the melted butter (not too hot), salt and beaten egg. For this it is best to use a large, strong wooden spoon, beating until a dough is formed. Knead the dough on a lightly floured surface until smooth and elastic, 5–10 minutes. If the dough remains too moist and sticks to the fingers, it must be vigorously beaten again. If necessary you can gradually work in a little extra flour.

When the dough has been kneaded sufficiently, sprinkle with flour, cover with a damp cloth and leave to rise in a warm place until double in size. This is called the first rising. When well risen, knead lightly again and shape the dough to fit the prepared loaf tin, or form into individual bread rolls and place on a greased baking tray.

Before baking, the shaped dough must be risen again or proved. The tin or baking tray containing the dough should be put inside a large oiled polythene bag. The proving time depends on the temperature at which it takes place but is usually shorter than the first rising period. When placing the dough in a tin or mould, fill only halfway up with the dough and leave until it rises to the top of the tin. While the dough is proving preheat the oven to hot (230°C, 450°F, Gas Mark 8).

When proving the dough, fill the tin or mould only half-full, and then leave until the dough rises to the top of the tin.

Brush the bread with beaten egg yolk and finally place in the oven. Bake the large loaf for 35–45 minutes, the smaller loaves for 25–35 minutes, and the individual rolls for 15–20 minutes. The cooked loaf should be slightly shrunken from the sides of the tin and when turned out it should sound hollow when tapped on the bottom.

Pastries

Puff Pastry

Cook's Tips

• Allow frozen puff pastry to thaw out at room temperature for approximately 1 hour.
• Roll out puff pastry on a board which is only lightly floured. During rolling it is important to remember never to roll this type of pastry in one direction only, but in two directions, that is from top to bottom and from left to right. If rolled in one direction only it will not rise evenly during baking.
• Cut puff pastry with a very sharp knife, to prevent the edges sticking together. If using pastry cutters it is advisable to dip them in cold water before cutting out the pastry.
• When brushing puff pastry with egg yolk avoid the cut edges, or it will cause them to stick together and thus prevent the pastry layers from rising during baking.
• Puff pastry leftovers can be laid one upon the other, pressed firmly together and rolled out again. Small pieces and strips are suitable for decoration.
• Always place puff pastry on a baking tray or in a tin which has been lightly sprinkled with cold water, and leave to stand for 15 minutes before baking.

Shortcrust Pastry

If you follow the basic rules for making this pastry you can be sure of success. Shortcrust pastry is easy and quick to prepare, but extra time must be allowed for it to rest in the refrigerator before

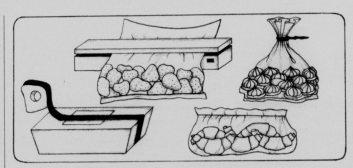

For sealing, ties or plastic clips or freezer tape which will resist frost are suitable, also the heat-sealing device for polythene bags.

Packaging Materials Available

Foil This material is particularly useful being in sheet form, as it can be moulded or shaped around the food to be frozen, making it completely airtight. It comes in two thicknesses, domestic and heavy duty, the latter being suitable for freezing purposes. Cakes which are thawed in their foil wrapping are at the same time well protected against drying out.

Foil containers These are extremely suitable for cakes, particularly uncooked cake mixtures, as they can be frozen and cooked in the same container. They are sold in various sizes and shapes; pie plates, basins, loaf tins, flan dishes and gussetted foil bags.

Polythene bags These fulfil almost all the requirements of an ideal freezer wrapper. With careful handling they can be used several times. For freezer use, polythene bags must be of thick gauge (200–250) to be moisture proof. The much thinner bags are suitable only for keeping food fresh. If using bags for freezing several times, test well before using to ensure there is no hole in the bag, no matter how small (test by filling with water). After use, wash well in detergent, rinse several times in hot water and hang up to dry. This material should be sealed with a heat-sealing device, rubber bands, plastic or metal clips, or with sealing tape.

Polythene containers These must be able to withstand sub-zero temperatures without cracking or warping. The seal must be airtight. Make sure that you buy reputable makes as cheaper containers will not last for very long.

Sheet wrapping This comes in the form of polythene sheets or cling film. Polythene sheeting requires sealing with freezer tape or a heat sealer, whereas film will cling itself automatically. Cling film comes in two thicknesses, one for short term freezing and freezer film for long term storage. Its advantage is that it is invaluable for wrapping irregular shapes, and it also makes frozen food easily recognisable.

Other packagings Yogurt, cream and butter containers can also be used for freezing when cleaned thoroughly. They are suitable for biscuit crumbs, raw cake mixture, egg whites or whipped cream. Always be careful not to fill these containers to the brim.

Sealing For this, depending on the type of packaging, rubber bands, ties or plastic clips, or freezer tape which will resist frost are all suitable, and also the heat-sealing device which gives polythene bags an airtight seal.

Labelling Every container, no matter how small, should be labelled. On the label you must note the contents, freezing date and any special characteristics such as 'halved fruit', 'whole fruit', etc. Either use the self-sticking labels which withstand cold, or sealing tape which you can write on. Write with a ball-point or felt-tip pen. There are also special marker pens which will write directly on to foil or plastic.

Whichever packaging material you choose, it is important that the air is expelled before sealing and that the material is pulled tight (with the exception of yeast dough – this expands slightly in the freezer, so the wrapping should be loosely sealed). With foil you expel the air by pressing firmly and folding the edges over double. Only use foil once for freezing, then use it for covering or keeping food fresh in the refrigerator. With each time of using the foil, small, barely visible tears are formed which, if used again, would cause the food to dry out. With bags suck out the air with a straw or a vacuum pump. Never fill boxes, beakers or jars too full as the frozen food will expand slightly; leave 2·5 cm/1 inch clear at the top. If necessary secure lids with freezer tape. Boxes without lids should be covered with foil folded double and the foil then fastened down firmly with a rubber band.

Food Freezing Chart

Food	Storage Time	Hints on Packaging	Thawing Hints
Yeast and Yeast Doughs			
Fresh yeast	Up to 6 months	Divide into 15 g/½ oz or 30 g/1 oz portions, wrap in freezer film and store in an airtight container.	Allow to thaw at room temperature for 1–2 hours and use as required.
Small yeast cakes e.g. doughnuts and croissants	Up to 4 months	Freeze cooked or uncooked. If freezing raw dough, place in an oiled polythene bag, leaving enough space for expansion.	Thaw cooked food at room temperature, wrap in foil to prevent drying out and reheat in a moderate oven. Thaw raw dough at room temperature and shape as required.
Large yeast cakes e.g. Kugelhopf	Up to 4 months	Wrap in a polythene bag or freezer film.	Thaw at room temperature, wrap in foil and reheat in a moderate oven.
Pizza	Up to 3 months	Freeze the shaped raw dough bases, with a sheet of greaseproof between each one, and pack in a polythene bag, *or* freeze baked.	Top with chosen filling whilst frozen and bake immediately in a hot oven. Thaw the baked pizza at room temperature and reheat in a moderately hot oven, wrapped in foil.
Bread rolls	Up to 3 months	Pack in polythene bags.	Wrap in aluminium foil and place still frozen in a moderately hot oven. Reheat until thawed thoroughly.

The Art of Baking

Food Freezing Chart

Food	Storage Time	Hints on Packaging	Thawing Hints
Pastries			
Puff pastry (uncooked)	3 months	Wrap in freezer film and place in a polythene bag.	Thaw in a refrigerator overnight, or at room temperature. Use as required.
Puff pastry (cooked)	4–6 months	Open freeze and store in a rigid polythene container.	Thaw at room temperature and reheat in a moderate oven.
Shortcrust pastry (uncooked)	3 months	Pack in usable quantities in freezer film and place in a polythene bag.	Thaw in a refrigerator overnight or at room temperature. Use as required.
Shortcrust pastry (cooked)	4–6 months	Open freeze and pack in rigid polythene containers. (Flan and tartlet cases are better frozen baked but unfilled.)	Thaw at room temperature.
Sweet or savoury filled and baked flans	Up to 3 months	Wrap in freezer film and place in a rigid polythene container. Individual slices can be wrapped in freezer film and frozen as above.	Allow to thaw overnight in a refrigerator and crisp up in a moderately hot oven if to be served hot.
Choux pastry	4–6 months	(*a*) Uncooked paste – pack in a rigid polythene container.	Thaw in the refrigerator overnight.
		(*b*) Uncooked paste – pipe on to greaseproof paper and open freeze, then pack into rigid polythene containers.	Thaw in the refrigerator overnight or at room temperature, then bake according to the recipe.
		(*c*) Baked, but unfilled – slightly undercook, open freeze and pack in rigid polythene containers.	Allow to thaw and crisp up in a moderately hot oven.
Cakes and Biscuits			
Whisked sponge cake	Up to 3 months	Interleave the sponge layers with greaseproof paper and pack in a polythene bag.	Thaw at room temperature, fill and decorate as liked.
		Can be frozen filled and decorated; open freeze and pack in a rigid polythene container.	Thaw at room temperature.
Swiss roll	Up to 3 months	Freeze filled wrapped in freezer film or a polythene bag.	Thaw at room temperature.
Meringues (unfilled)	4–6 months	Open freeze, then pack in rigid polythene containers.	Thaw at room temperature and fill as required.
Basic sandwich cake	Up to 3 months	As for whisked sponge cake.	Thaw at room temperature.
Cheesecake	Up to 3 months	Freeze whole or in slices. Wrap individual slices in freezer film.	Thaw overnight in the refrigerator.
Biscuits (baked)	Up to 3 months	Wrap in polythene bags.	Thaw 2–3 hours at room temperature.
Biscuits (unbaked)	4–6 months	Wrap dough in freezer film.	Thaw 2–3 hours at room temperature then bake.
Fillings and Icings			
Double cream, whipped	Up to 6 months	Add a little icing sugar to act as a stabiliser and store in a rigid polythene container *or* pipe on to greaseproof paper and open freeze before packing in a rigid polythene container.	Thaw overnight in the refrigerator. Use almost immediately.
Custard butter cream	Up to 3 months	Store in a rigid polythene container.	Thaw 2–3 hours at room temperature.
French butter cream	Up to 3 months	Store in a rigid polythene container.	Thaw 2–3 hours at room temperature.

Index

239